Penguin Education

Penguin Modern Economics Texts
General Editor: B. J. McCormick

Industrial Economics
Editor: H. Townsend

Nationalized Industries
Graham L. Reid and Kevin Allen

Graham L. Reid and Kevin Allen

Nationalized Industries

Penguin Education

Penguin Education
Penguin Books Ltd,
Harmondsworth, Middlesex, England
Penguin Books Inc., 7110 Ambassador Road,
Baltimore, Md 21207, U S A
Penguin Books Australia Ltd, Ringwood,
Victoria, Australia
Penguin Books Canada Ltd, 41 Steelcase Road West,
Markham, Ontario, Canada
Penguin Books (N.Z.) Ltd, 182–190 Wairau Road,
Auckland 10, New Zealand

First published 1970
Reprinted 1971
Reprinted with corrections 1973
Reprinted 1975

Copyright © Graham L. Reid and Kevin Allen, 1970

Made and printed in Great Britain by
C. Nicholls & Company Ltd
Set in Monotype Times

Penguin Modern Economics Texts

This volume is one in a series of unit texts designed to reduce the price of knowledge for students of economics in universities and colleges of higher education. The units may be used singly or in combination with other units to form attractive and unusual teaching programmes. The volumes will cover the major teaching areas but they will differ from conventional books in their attempt to chart and explore new directions in economic thinking. The traditional divisions of theory and applied, of positive and normative and of micro and macro will tend to be blurred as authors impose new and arresting ideas on the traditional corpus of economics. Some units will fall into conventional patterns of thought but many will transgress established beliefs.

Penguin Modern Economic Texts are published in units in order to achieve certain objectives. First, a large range of short texts at inexpensive prices gives the teacher flexibility in planning his course and recommending texts for it. Secondly, the pace at which important new work is published requires the project to be adaptable. Our plan allows a unit to be revised or a fresh unit to be added with maximum speed and minimal cost to the reader.

The international range of authorship will, it is hoped, bring out the richness and diversity in economic analysis and thinking.

B. J. MCC.

Contents

Editorial Foreword

Nationalized industries occupy a peculiar place in economic discussion. Much of the time it is as if they do not exist at all; analysis runs in terms of a private enterprise economy where undertakings are all owned by proprietors or shareholders. At other times they exist, but only as imaginary entities. They are thought of as identical with one another, experiencing decreasing average costs as output increases and unresponsive demand whatever price is charged, all having always been organized as they happen to be at the moment, and all monopolies. Sometimes they are seen as they are, and this is how Allen and Reid present them.

There is much to be said for seeing the nationalized industries plain, because they have been the scene of some of the most instructive events in post-war industry. Electricity supply is a case study in continuous growth, rapid technological change and economies of scale. Here is an industry where the capacity of basic units of plant has multiplied seventeenfold in twenty years. Gas supply has been the scene of equally dramatic technological advance, changing from coal to naphtha, and from naphtha to natural gas, within a decade. The coal industry has demonstrated the way in which an industry may be contracted and labour redeployed with a minimum of suffering.

The fuel and power industries have been the scene of competition between themselves, and also between these industries and the oil industry. But this has been competition between the big battalions. In road haulage, we have gained experience of a mixed system of industrial organization, with private undertakings and nationalized ones competing with one another, whilst the scale of production has varied greatly from one road transport activity to another. The contraction of rail transport contrasts with the contraction of coal and provides a complementary subject for study. Air transport provides the opportunity to investigate the activities of an international cartel.

Kevin Allen and Graham L. Reid are well qualified to apply economic analysis within the nationalized sector. Reid has been a Senior Lecturer in Applied Economics and Allen is a Lecturer in Applied Economics, both at the University of Glasgow. At Glasgow, they have both been concerned with a large research project on the working of the nationalized industries.

H. T.

Acknowledgements

This book is part of a larger study on the economics of the nationalized industries presently being carried out in the Department of Social and Economic Research with the help of a grant from the Carnegie Trust. Our colleagues in the Department have given us valuable assistance and comments, and we are most grateful to M. C. MacLennan, L. C. Hunter, D. J. Harris and A. W. J. Thomson. We are also indebted to the Editorial Board for advice throughout the preparation of the book. All errors of fact and judgement remain our own responsibility.

G.L.R.
K.A.

1 Introduction

The word 'nationalization' has very strong political overtones which are sometimes allowed to obscure the fact that the nationalized industries exist for the same purpose as any privately owned business, namely to provide goods or services for which there is a demand. Although the industries are similar to private enterprise in their basic aim, they differ in other respects. For one thing, they are very much larger than the average privately owned company and often have a considerable degree of monopoly power. Also, the political background against which they operate cannot be ignored. Because they are publicly owned, the nationalized industries are accountable to Parliament and are subject to political influence and control. Most important from our point of view, the economics of the nationalized industries present some interesting special problems, and in this book we have set ourselves the task of examining some of these economic problems as they have affected six industries: the electricity industry, the gas industry, the coal industry, the railways, the nationalized road haulage industry and the airlines.

Each industry is dealt with in a separate chapter, and in this Introduction we take a more comprehensive view of two major questions. Section 1 illustrates the importance of the nationalized industries in the economy, while section 2 outlines the changing view of policy towards the nationalized industries. One of the major economic problems has been to develop a policy of economic control of the nationalized industries so that they use resources efficiently, and section 2 illustrates very briefly how a policy of this kind had developed by the later 1960s. Finally, section 3 explains in more detail our method of approach in the industry chapters.

1. Nationalized Industries in the Public Sector

How important are the nationalized industries in the economy today? Table 1 gives some comparable data for the year 1966/7, for a selection of nationalized industries.

Table 1
Selected Data on the Nationalized Industries: Financial Year up to March 1967

	Average net assets	Net income[1]	Net income as per cent of net assets	Fixed invest- ment	Employ- ment
	£m	£m	Per cent	£m	Thousands
Post Office	1584	126·5	8·0	266·4	422
National Coal Board	794[2]	29·0	3·7	89·9	492
Electricity (E & W)	3876	200·4	5·1	664·8	229
North of Scotland Hydro-Electric Board	258	12·8	5·0	9·9	4
South of Scotland Electricity Board	316	14·7	4·6	47·1	16
Gas Council and Boards	966	46·5	4·8	215·0	124
British Overseas Airways Corporation	134	29·0	21·7	11·8	19
British European Airways	102	4·8	4·8	17·1	20
British Airports Authority	54	5·6	10·3	7·0	3
British Railways Board[3]	1931	−70·2	−3·6	106·8	361
London Transport Board[3]	218	1·1	0·5	22·1	74

	Average net assets	Net income[1]	Net income as per cent of net assets	Fixed invest-ment	Employ-ment
	£m	£m	Per cent	£m	Thousands
British Transport Docks Board[3]	95	5·1	5·4	9·8	11
British Waterways[3]	13	−0·6	−4·9	1·0	3
Transport Holding Co., of which:	175	14·3	8·2	23·3	103
(Road Haulage)	(78)	(4·9)	(6·9)	(14·6)	(38)
Total, all industries	10,516	419·0	3·9	1492·0	1881
Total six industries	*8455*	*271·9*	*3·2*	*1177·0*	*1303*

Notes: 1. Net income is trading surplus and other income less depreciation and foreseeable obsolescence.

2. This reflects only part of the capital reconstruction under the Coal Industry Act, 1965. See chapter 4.

3. These data refer to the calendar year 1966.

Source: Select Committee on Nationalized Industries (1968), *Ministerial Control of the Nationalized Industries*, HMSO, vol. 3, p. 2.

The six industries covered by the following chapters are italicized, and a comparison between the last two lines of the table shows that these six industries accounted for almost 85 per cent of the net assets of the nationalized industries and about two thirds of their employment. The Post Office, steel, and London Transport are the only nationalized industries of any size not covered by this book. The first two became public corporations only in 1967–9, and the last ceased to be nationalized when the control of London's transport network was vested in the Greater London Council.

The totals in Table 1 give some indication of the overall importance of the nationalized industries. In employment terms, their total of 1·9 million was about 7 per cent of the total working population, equal to about 22 per cent of the number working in manufacturing industry. The National Coal Board, the Post Office and British Railways were the three largest employers in the world outside the United States. The nationalized industries contributed about 10 per cent of gross domestic product in 1967, and their capital requirements were enormous. Their fixed investment of £1492 million was between one-quarter and one-fifth of total gross domestic fixed capital formation, and was higher than the total for the whole of manufacturing industry.[1] In addition, the nationalized industries' share of both total fixed investment and public investment has been increasing. It is therefore important that these industries be efficient and profitable, and that departures from profitable operation for social reasons be thoroughly justified. This can be well illustrated by the fact that

in Exchequer terms a decline of only 1 per cent in the earning power of the industries as a whole means an increase of £90 million per annum to be found by taxation or Exchequer borrowing – approximately equal to 2½p on the standard rate of income tax.[2]

The nationalized industries occupy a key position in the economy not only in themselves, but also because of the profound effect they can have on the efficient operation of the rest of the economy. For example, except for oil, the energy sector is nationalized and the price of fuel to the domestic and industrial consumer depends on the efficiency of the coal, electricity and gas industries. In the transport sector, the operations of the nationalized industries are vital to the economy. The railways carry a great deal of the long-distance passenger and heavy freight traffic, while the nationalized road haulage undertakings are the largest units in the road haulage industry. Similarly, the nationalized airlines control the greater part of

1. One may note that, using net assets as a measure of size, the electricity industry is the largest undertaking in Britain, and is about two and a half times the size of I C I.

2. Select Committee on Nationalised Industries (1968), *Ministerial Control of the Nationalised Industries*, H M S O, vol. 2, p. 1.

the British civil aviation industry. As well as these industries, there are other areas where the efficiency of publicly owned industry is essential. The nationalized British Steel Corporation accounts for 85 per cent of steel output, while the Post Office has a monopoly of postal services and telecommunications.

In view of their central position in the economy and of the very considerable call on resources which they make, it is important that the industries should aim at a high level of economic efficiency, since inefficiency will impose costs on the consumer, on industry and on the community in general. However, as the next section illustrates, policy towards the nationalized industries has not always been clearly directed towards ensuring an efficient use of resources.

2. The Changing View of the Nationalized Industries

Most of the nationalized industries were not taken into public ownership primarily for economic reasons, though there has often been an attempt to include an economic rationale in the decision to nationalize a particular industry. Some of the industries were natural or statutory monopolies, e.g. electricity, gas and railways, and had to be subject to a quite strict degree of public control, but public control and public ownership are by no means the same thing. In Britain, public utilities and the railways were highly regulated by statute for many years before they were actually nationalized, and in many other countries such industries as civil aviation, railways, gas, electricity and telecommunications remain privately owned though publicly controlled. The initial reason for nationalization has been political rather than economic, and although the re-nationalization of steel in 1968/9 and the proposed nationalization of the docks in 1970/71 was to be carried out ostensibly to rationalize the industries and to make them more efficient, it is an open question whether this aim could not have been fulfilled by a different method of control rather than by outright public ownership.

In the period 1945–51, when the fuel and power industries, the railways and road haulage were nationalized, there was little attempt to spell out in detail the economic benefits of nationalization, and there was no attempt to develop a set of economic criteria for the way in which the industries should be run. There was a statutory requirement that the industries should break even, taking one year with another, after making proper provision for depreciation, but the application of this simple financial rule was not enough to guarantee efficient use of resources. There was little or no guidance from the government on the economic policies the industries ought to follow in their attempt to break even. The lack of any systematic method of economic control of the nationalized industries showed itself in many ways, and three in particular may be singled out here.

Firstly, the industries were given no real guidance on the type of pricing policy they ought to follow. Their statutory obligations prevented them from discriminating against any consumer or group of consumers, and this was often taken as justification for charging prices which were not closely related to costs. There was a tendency towards pricing on the basis of average costs, under which consumers paid much the same price per unit in spite of the fact that there were substantially different costs in supplying different consumers. For example, all rail passengers paid the same fare per mile in spite of the fact that stopping-train services cost many times more to provide than long-distance express services. The fact that prices were not firmly based on costs meant that unprofitable areas of business were cross-subsidized by profitable areas, and so long as an industry broke even there was no particular economic incentive to cut back unprofitable sectors. Indeed, there were strong political pressures for the maintenance at relatively low prices of services which were unprofitable but thought to be 'socially desirable': this was particularly the case in railways, coal and airlines.

Secondly, the control and appraisal of capital investment was inadequate. Some of the industries were capable of absorbing enormous amounts of capital, most of it raised by Government loans rather than through the capital market. If this capital was not used efficiently and profitably there could be a very considerable misallocation of resources, but no clear method existed in some of the industries of evaluating capital projects (see the discussion in chapter 5 of the railways' modernization plan). As a result, decisions on which projects should be undertaken and on how much should be invested were often taken without sufficient economic analysis, either by the industries or by the controlling Government departments.

Thirdly, in the framing of overall policies, the industries tended to be regarded as independent entities. It is rather paradoxical that 'co-ordination' should have been one of the watchwords in the early days of nationalization, since where co-ordination was attempted it was generally only in physical rather than economic terms. For example, the British Transport Commission was set up in 1947 to co-ordinate freight and passenger road and rail transport, but the B.T.C.'s methods centred round licences and physical allocation, and there was never any attempt to establish a foundation of economic co-ordination, nor was there a proper appreciation of what would constitute the most efficient allocation of resources within the transport sector.

Policy towards the nationalized industries continued to lack a firm economic foundation throughout the 1950s, and though the need for reorganization and change was recognized, there were political and social difficulties in dealing with the problems which the industries were facing. One such difficulty was that nationalization and the nationalized industries were issues of ideology in party politics. Opponents of nationalization tended to attribute the industries' problems to the simple fact that they were nationalized, while supporters of nationalization defended the industries' economic shortcomings on social and political grounds. Though it was obvious that most of the industries would never be returned to private ownership by any Government, it was none the less difficult for rational economic discussion to proceed on the basis that the industries existed and would continue to exist as an important part of the economy and so ought to be run as efficiently as possible. The railway industry provides a good example of how social and political considerations could influence economic policy. Throughout the latter half of the 1950s, the deficit of the railways accumulated to an alarming degree, and the scale of the problem was so huge that it would have been difficult to tackle under any conditions. Part of the solution to the railways' difficulties would have been the withdrawal of railway services to particular groups of people and particular areas, but the social and political price was simply too high for any Government to pay. Similarly, the rundown of the coal industry has particularly affected certain groups and areas, to which special attention has had to be paid (see chapter 4). However, during the 1950s, the main difficulty in tackling the problems of the nationalized industries was not simply the primacy of political issues, but the fact that changes were not based on an economic framework of control.

Since the publication of the White Paper on *The Financial and Economic Objectives of the Nationalised Industries* (Cmnd 1337) in April 1961, a new framework of control has been developed. The Government has formulated a series of rules or guidelines within which the nationalized industries ought to operate in the interests of achieving an efficient use of resources.[1] These guidelines are a partial substitute for the market constraints which affect a firm operating in a competitive environment. They are quite specific about the type of pricing policy that the industries should use, the minimum rate of return which new investment projects should show and the method of evaluating such projects, and the overall rate of return on net assets which the industries' whole operations should achieve. There are certain theoretical and practical problems in the formulation and application of these guidelines as the industry chapters will show, but these cannot be discussed here.[2] The point is, however, that the guidelines constitute a particular type of economic framework, and give a

1. The latest expression of these guidelines can be found in *Nationalised Industries: A Review of Economic and Financial Objectives* (1967), Cmnd 3437, H.M.S.O.

2. See *Ministerial Control of the Nationalised Industries*, vol. 1, chs. 5 and 6.

set of rules by which the performance of the industry can be judged. As a result, where the principles laid down under the guidelines cannot be adhered to, or where the State decides for political and/or social reasons that the industries should operate in a non-commercial fashion, the departure from the rules can be appreciated. Thus, for example, the railways' 'socially justifiable' services are separately identified and financed, and the electricity industry's obligation to use extra coal is compensated by the Government.

A second consequence of the changed view of the nationalized industries and the stress on their economic efficiency within the guidelines is that policy problems have come to be analysed from a wider point of view than that of the individual industry. To develop a policy which gives the best use of national resources necessitates a sectoral or multi-sectoral approach: one must take into account the effect of changes in one nationalized industry on other nationalized industries and on the private sector. For example, the exploitation of natural gas was planned in the context of the fuel sector as a whole and, in assessing the implications of this new energy source, the Ministry of Power considered the effects of exploitation policy on other areas of the economy (see chapter 3). Similarly, the Transport Act 1968 laid the basis for co-ordination of road and rail freight transport, and though the means of achieving co-ordination was partly by licensing, the objectives of the Act were worked out after considerable economic analysis as to which kind of policy mix would give the best use of resources in the transport sector, both public and private (see chapters 6 and 5). The sectoral approach recognizes that the nationalized industries are not independent entities. The industries are interdependent insofar as certain of them operate within the same sector and insofar as they all have an effect on parts of the private sector.

The 'new view' of the nationalized industries therefore has two important aspects. Firstly, it has led to the establishment of a set of guidelines or rules within which the industries should operate, and secondly, it recognizes that the industries cannot be treated as separate economic entities.

3. Our Approach to the Industries

In this book, the nationalized industries are treated as economic undertakings which use resources to produce goods and services, and the economic problems of the industries are examined. The development of each industry is explained to show how it reached its position in 1968, the economic situation which it faced is outlined, and the likely future problems and prospects for each industry are considered. Each chapter therefore deals with such topics as the structure of production, output, costs and prices, investment, manpower and productivity, technological change, and financial performance. The individual topics are not of equal importance in all the industries and are consequently discussed in varying degrees of detail.

In the space available, we have had to be severely selective in our treatment of the industries, and many interesting and important areas have had to be ignored or dealt with in summary fashion. Firstly, the industry chapters do not generally deal with the long-term historical development of the industries, with the political and social arguments lying behind nationalization, with the political background to the control and accountability of the industries, or with the administration of the industries. However, where these topics are essential to an understanding of the current or future economic problems, they are introduced.

Secondly, we deal with the economics of the nationalized industries, rather than with the economics of public enterprise. As the previous section has indicated, there are theoretical and practical problems in developing guidelines or rules for the operation of public enterprise, particularly in respect of efficient pricing and investment policies. The industry chapters, however, limit themselves to considering the performance and problems of the specific industries within the framework of the guidelines, rather than to the theoretical problem of establishing the guidelines themselves.

Thirdly, though the industries are treated separately, the chapters acknowledge the importance of taking a sectoral view.

Thus in the coal industry chapter we have introduced the effect of other fuels on the demand for coal, while the railway and road haulage chapters try to bring out the interdependence of these industries. In general, where some aspect of one industry's operations has been affected by the operations of another, the discussion covers both industries so as to make their relationship clear.

Finally, the period 1968–9 in a sense represented a threshold for most of the nationalized industries. Though the industries have been changing and developing ever since they were nationalized, particularly during the 1960s, at no time in the past were so many of the industries simultaneously affected by quite radical changes as in 1968–9. These changes had a number of causes: some were the result of technological factors, others were the accelerated application or effect of previous policies, while still others were economic, financial or administrative changes stemming from the new structure of economic control. The main changes in 1968–9 may be summarized as follows: the *gas industry* began the rapid build-up and distribution of natural gas from the North Sea; the *railways* and the *road haulage industry* began operating under the entirely new structure of the Transport Act 1968; the *airlines* saw the publication of the Edwards Committee Report with its recommendations for the future development of civil aviation; the *coal industry*'s closure and concentration policy began to be more deeply felt.

Since the book was written in 1968–69 there have been several new phases of policy. There was a good deal of discussion about de-nationalization and introducing more competition into the nationalized industries, and in 1971–72 the industries were seriously affected by Government price restraint and anti-inflationary policies. Although the basic economic problems of the industries remain as they were in 1968–69, we have taken the opportunity of revising sections of each chapter from the standpoint of late 1972.

2 The Electricity Industry

The electricity industry is one of Britain's major industries. It is a big employer of labour with a labour force of almost a quarter of a million, and has an enormous appetite for capital. Its total net assets in 1967 were some £4000 million and annual capital expenditure in the mid-1960s was running at over £550 million. It is an important part of the fuel sector in that it satisfies a large proportion of final energy demand[1] but it is also important in that it makes heavy demands on other fuel sectors. Its decision on what fuel to burn has important consequences for the other fuel industries, and this has not always been an advantage. The industry has two important characteristics. Firstly, the demand for its product varies considerably over the period of a day and between seasons. Secondly, the product cannot be stored in bulk. These characteristics, combined with the fact that production is capital-intensive, give rise to most of the industry's problems and fashion many of its policies.

This chapter is in five sections. Section 1 covers three aspects of demand – its growth, structure and fluctuations. Section 2 is concerned with supply and discusses the industry's organization and costs. Section 3 is a discussion of pricing policy in the industry. Section 4 covers the financial performance of the industry over the past six years, and the chapter concludes with a brief discussion of the possible future trends and developments in the industry.

1. Final energy demand excludes fuels used in the production of other fuels, e.g. coal in the production of electricity. Consumption of electricity in 1967, calculated in tons of coal equivalent, was nearly three times the consumption of gas.

1. Demand for Electricity

The demand for electricity has risen rapidly in the postwar period, from 45,500 GWh in 1950 to 90,500 GWh in 1959 and 161,700 GWh in 1967.[1] The rate of growth of demand slackened off in the mid-1960s. While it had been rising by just over 9·4 per cent per annum between 1953 and 1963, the annual rate of increase fell to around 5·5 per cent between 1963 and 1967. The main reasons for this slackening of the growth rate were the heavy retrenchment of the economy combined with large price increases and, to some extent, increased competition from the gas industry.

The growth of demand over the post-war period was rapid in all three major electricity consuming sectors, though demand from the domestic and commercial consumers grew faster than industrial demand, and the latter, in consequence, became a less important component of total demand. Table 2 shows the growth of electricity sales between 1951 and 1967 and the changing relative importance of the main consuming sectors.

The group 'industrial' sales in Table 2 covers a considerable range of industries. The main industrial markets, however, and the ones from which most of the growth came, are iron and steel, engineering and other metal trades, and chemical and allied trades. In 1967 these three industries accounted for almost 55 per cent of sales to industry. The greater part of these sales are for power and lighting purposes. In general, only where electricity has a technical advantage over other fuels, e.g. controllability, cleanliness, is it used for heating purposes. The growth of industrial sales would have been greater had it not been for the quite considerable growth of electricity generation by firms themselves. This is not covered in Table 2 which only includes sales by the nationalized sector.

1. The normal measure of power or capacity in electricity generation is the kilowatt (kW). One thousand kilowatts equal one megawatt (MW), and one million kilowatts equal one gigawatt (GW). The measures of energy or power consumed are the kilowatt hour (kWh), the megawatt hour (MWh) and the gigawatt hour (GWh).

Private generation by industry increased from 11,449 GWh in 1955 to 17,499 GWh in 1967. In 1967 this was about one-quarter the size of the nationalized electricity industry's sales to industry.

Table 2
Electricity Sales 1951 and 1967: Great Britain

	1951		1967		Percentage growth 1951–67
	G Wh	Per cent	G Wh	Per cent	
Industrial	25,350	50·2	67,446	41·7	166·1
Domestic	14,445	28·6	61,334	37·9	324·6
Commercial	6354	12·6	26,254	16·2	313·2
Other*	4364	8·6	6630	4·1	51·9
Total	50,513	100·0	161,664	100·0	220·0

* In order of importance, this group covers farms, traction (principally railways) and public lighting.

Source: Ministry of Power, *Statistical Digest 1967*.

Table 2 also shows the rapid growth of domestic sales since 1951 and their importance in total demand. About 75 per cent of domestic consumption is for cooking, water heating and space heating, and a similarly large proportion of the growth in domestic demand has arisen from these uses. Rising incomes and the growing popularity of domestic central heating, the advantages of electricity in terms of cleanliness, convenience and flexibility, good advertising aimed at depicting electricity as a 'modern' fuel plus the lack of competition from gas up to the early 1960s, are all factors which have contributed to the rapid growth of domestic demand for electricity.

One of the major problems which the industry has to face arises out of the fact that the demand for electricity is not constant over the period of a day or year. Firstly, the average level of demand in winter is about 60 per cent above that in summer. Secondly, there is a demand plateau between about 8·30 a.m.

and 9 p.m. on an average day which is about 50 per cent above demand in the night-time period. Thirdly, there are minor, but very important, peaks of demand at particular times of the day. These last between 9 a.m. and midday on a typical summer's day and 5.30–6 p.m. on a typical winter's day. These peaks are around 15 per cent above the normal day-time plateau of demand and take place when heavy domestic demand coincides with heavy industrial demand. Finally, the industry also suffers erratic peaking of demand during periods of abnormally cold weather. Some of these fluctuations in demand are of short duration, but electricity cannot be stored in bulk, and so the industry has to have adequate capacity to meet the severe peaks even though some of that capacity is used only infrequently. In 1967/8 the industry aimed at keeping a margin of 14 per cent over normal winter loads (17 per cent by 1970/71) in order to meet abnormal winter peaks.[1] Obviously the cost of supplying peak demand is very high, and the next section deals with some of the problems of supply.

2. The Supply of Electricity

The organizational arrangements for the supply of electricity differ between Scotland, and England and Wales. In Scotland there are two Boards, the South of Scotland Electricity Board which covers an area south of a line between Helensburgh in the west and the Firth of Tay in the east, and the North of Scotland Hydro-Electric Board which serves the rest of Scotland. Both Boards are responsible for the generation, transmission

1. The margin is not enough to provide complete protection against load shedding (voltage reductions) or load cutting (power cut). The industry has adopted a policy of not cutting voltage beyond 5 per cent, for reductions above this could endanger some electrical appliances. On the basis of probability calculations, it is estimated that a 17 per cent capacity margin will force the industry to shed load about twenty-four times a century and to cut load in some three years a century. To avoid load shedding completely would need a margin of about 40 per cent. It is interesting, if irrelevant, that if all the electrical appliances in Britain were switched on simultaneously, they would demand around seven times as much power as the industry could provide at maximum output!

and retail distribution of electricity in their individual areas. The north of Scotland is self-sufficient in electricity and indeed exports a small amount to the south of Scotland. The latter also imports power from England, and buys electricity from the Atomic Energy Authority nuclear station at Chapelcross. Imports and purchases amounted to about 18 per cent of total sales in the year ending March 1968.

The organization of electricity supply in England and Wales is quite different from that in Scotland. The industry is organized around three bodies. One is the Electricity Council whose task is to shape general policy and act as adviser to the relevant Minister on matters affecting the industry, and to promote and assist the maintenance and development of an efficient, co-ordinated and economical system of electricity supply. Secondly, there is the Central Electricity Generating Board (C.E.G.B.) which operates power stations and main transmission lines. The generating sector is divided administratively into five regions – North-East, North-West, Midlands, South-East and South-West. The C.E.G.B. sells electricity in bulk to the third group in the trinity, the twelve Area Electricity Boards which have responsibility for the distribution network and retail sales of electricity. The C.E.G.B. and the Area Boards are represented on the Electricity Council.[1]

The major aim of the electricity industry is to produce electricity at the lowest possible cost. In order to do this the industry needs first to use its existing capacity in the most economic manner, and secondly, to select the most economic method of generation when considering investment in new capacity or the renewal of existing capacity. These two aspects are discussed in turn below.

There are two main types of power stations, conventional or thermal power stations and nuclear power stations. Two other types of power station, gas turbine or internal combus-

1. In 1969 a new structure was proposed to increase the centralized control of the industry. A new Electricity Authority was to be responsible for the over-all development of the industry and the control of capital investment. These legislative proposals lapsed with the change of government in 1970.

tion engines and hydro-electric stations, are very much less important. In the two main types the principle of generation is the same; water is heated to produce steam and the steam drives turbines to produce electricity. Conventional stations use coal or oil as the source of heat, while nuclear stations use a controlled nuclear reaction. These different types of power stations have different patterns of costs as we shall see later. For the moment, it is sufficient to note that the running costs of internal combustion and gas turbine stations are higher than those of conventional coal- or oil-fired stations which are, in turn, higher than those of nuclear stations. Within these three groups there are further differences in running costs between individual stations.

The economic performance of a conventional station depends on the steam conditions (pressure and temperature) for which it was designed, its capacity, age and fuel costs per ton. Newer stations and bigger stations generally have higher thermal efficiencies[1] and lower running costs. Better design and metallurgical advances, making possible higher pressures, temperatures, and greater size of stations and sets (boiler and turbine units, usually up to four in a station), have made for considerable improvement in station thermal efficiencies in the post-war period. Station thermal efficiency increased from an average 21·6 per cent in 1950 to 27·9 per cent in 1967. Little advance was made between 1962 when the level was 27·5 per cent, and 1967, largely as a result of technical difficulties with the boilers and turbines in some of the big 500 MW sets and the need to use older, less efficient sets and stations more intensively.

The conventional station with the best thermal efficiency in 1967/8 was the Ferrybridge C station, commissioned in that year, which had a thermal efficiency of 34·57 per cent. This is a 2000 MW station with four 500 MW sets. But coming down the list, the industry also had (in 1966/7) forty conventional stations of below 25 MW capacity each of which had average thermal efficiencies of less than 16 per cent. The works

1. The thermal efficiency of a station power is the calorific value or heat output of electricity sent out as a percentage of the calorific value or heat output of the total fuel consumed.

cost or running cost per kWh sent out (excluding capital costs) was very high for these inefficient stations. Table 3 shows the works costs per kWh and the thermal efficiency of stations of selected sizes in 1966/7, and it is clear that in spite of the over-all improvement in average thermal efficiency since the war, the industry was holding capacity of quite differing efficiencies and costs.

Table 3
Works Cost and Thermal Efficiency of Conventional Stations by Size, 1966/7: Great Britain

Capacity MW	Average thermal efficiency per cent	Works cost in pence of generation per kWh sent out
5 and under 10	9·0	7·265 (3·03p)
20 and under 25	15·9	2·374 (0·99p)
100 and under 150	23·0	1·016 (0·42p)
300 and under 400	28·6	0·697 (0·29p)
600 and over	32·6	0·574 (0·24p)
Average (all conventional stations)	27·7	0·739 (0·31p)

Source: Ministry of Power, *Statistical Digest 1967*.

It is important to appreciate that the electricity industry is an inter-connected system, and that as demand on the system increases it is met by bringing additional stations into operation. These stations need not be in the area of demand. Electricity can be transmitted on high-voltage lines so that increased demand in one area can be met by the output of power stations in another, though of course there are power losses and therefore costs in transmission. Obviously, then, if the industry wishes to minimize the cost of satisfying demand, it will try to avoid using the higher-cost stations, and in order to minimize its costs, stations are brought into operation according to the merit order system. This involves ranking stations according to fuel costs, which represent about six-sevenths of running costs, and using them according to their ranking. The process can be described thus:

As the demand for electricity builds up over any period it is satisfied first by the lowest fuel cost stations, then by the next cheapest stations and so on. The principle being that the demand for electricity should be met with the least commitment of additional resources.[1]

The system is such that nuclear stations with their very low running costs are always used on base-load, i.e. to meet the basic demand on the system, and are never switched on and off to meet seasonal or daily peak demands. In fact there would be technical problems in doing this, but the low running costs of nuclear stations make them exceptionally suitable for base-load operation, and they are used very intensively. In 1966/7 they had a plant load factor of 68·07 per cent as against the average plant load factor of 46·43 per cent for all stations in Great Britain.[2] The merit order system also meant intensive use of the large lower-cost conventional stations, and in 1966/7 conventional stations of 500–600 MW had an average plant load factor of 72·84 per cent.[3] By contrast, small high-cost stations below 25 MW were only used for peak demand and had plant load factors of less than 10 per cent. The relatively infrequent use of the less economic stations, arising out of the merit order system, is well illustrated by the fact that while stations of below 100 MW accounted for about 20 per cent

1. Webb, M. G. (1967), 'Some principles involved in the economic comparison of power stations', *Manchester School of Social and Economic Studies*, vol. 35, p. 1.

2. Plant load factor is the average hourly quantity of electricity sent out during the year expressed as a percentage of the average output capacity of that plant during the year.

3. It is perhaps surprising that these conventional stations had higher plant load factors than the nuclear stations, but technical and maintenance problems can radically affect plant load factors: in 1965/6 nuclear stations had a higher plant load factor than 500–600 MW stations, at 73·22 per cent against 68·4 per cent. Another example of technical problems is the low load factor of 46·8 per cent in 1966/7 for stations of 600 MW and over. These experienced trouble with boilers and turbines and were unable to run as intensively as had been expected.

of conventional steam station capacity in 1966/7, they produced only about 7 per cent of total electricity sent out by conventional steam stations. Gas turbine stations and oil engine stations, having relatively high running costs, are also used only for peak-load generation and had plant load factors of 5·25 per cent and 21·07 per cent respectively.

The merit order system ensures that the high-cost stations are only brought into service in order to meet peaks in demand, and obviously the meeting of these peaks is very expensive even in terms of running costs. On top of these are the capital costs of the stations which, being spread over little output, are extremely high per unit. There is no satisfactory estimate available of the cost of supplying peak demand but much of it must be provided at a price well below the cost of catering for it.

The problems and cost of supplying peak demand over the period of a day could be considerably reduced if an economic method existed for the bulk storage of electricity. The only development in this direction has been the pumped storage stations of the type used at Ffestiniog and Loch Sloy. These hydro-electric stations store not the electricity itself, but the water with which it can be generated. The stations use an unusual form of reversible turbine which can act both as a pump and a generator. During the off-peak hours at night, electricity is used to pump water from a lower reservoir into a higher one, and during the day peak periods the water is allowed to flow back into the lower reservoir generating electricity as it falls. The economics of pumped storage rest heavily on a cheap source of off-peak power for pumping the water into the higher reservoir, and this generating method may have more relevance in the mid and late 1970s with the development of low-cost nuclear power than it does today. In any case, it can only cater for daily peaks or plateaux and can do little for the seasonal variations in demand. The problem of seasonal demand is common to all energy industries, but it is more serious for the electricity industry because of the capital-intensive nature of production and the lack of any economic method of long-term storage, either by the consumer or the industry itself.

The second major problem of the electricity industry in the field of supply concerns the longer-term problem of which generating method to use in new stations. The great majority of generating capacity currently available is coal-fired. At the end of 1966 about 73·7 per cent was coal-fired, 12·3 per cent oil- and dual-fired, 6·5 per cent nuclear and 7·5 per cent 'other'.[1] The greater part of the 'other' capacity (over 50 per cent) was hydro-electric plant, with gas turbines and a small amount of oil engine capacity making up the rest. Over 75 per cent of the hydro-electric capacity is in Scotland.

The major problem facing the industry in the context of new capacity is the choice between coal, oil and nuclear stations. Since the mid-1950s, when about 90 per cent of capacity was coal-fired, the building of nuclear and oil plants has inevitably cut down the proportion of coal-fired capacity. Nevertheless the vast majority of stations under construction in 1967 were coal burning. Out of a total 35,000 MW of plant under construction, 25,000 MW was coal-fired, 6000 MW oil- and dual-fired (coal and oil) and 4000 MW was nuclear.[2]

The development of oil-fired capacity and perhaps nuclear capacity would undoubtedly have been greater if it had not been for the protectionist policy towards coal. Oil-fired stations were penalized by the heavy oil duty amounting to 2.42d. (1p) a gallon in 1968, but even so these stations were competitive with all but the best coal-fired stations. The building of oil plant was further limited, however:

Policy in the last few years has been to limit new oil-fired stations to sites where they show exceptional cost advantages and not to allow the conversion of coal-fired stations to oil unless there were very special reasons, such as to stop serious air pollution.[3]

Though in 1968 the industry had more capacity in oil-fired

1. *Fuel Policy* (1967), HMSO, Cmnd 3438, p. 15. It should be noted that the figures are for capacity. As a result of operating the merit order system, the proportion of electricity *generated* by nuclear power, and to a slight extent oil-fired stations, is higher than the figures above. In 1966/7 about 9·4 per cent of electricity was generated by nuclear power and about 10·8 per cent in 1967/8.
2. ibid., p. 14
3. ibid., p. 16.

stations than in nuclear stations, nuclear power is usually seen as being the main competitor to coal-fired stations in the future. There are three types of nuclear station. Firstly, there is the Magnox type – nine stations, all generating by 1972, having a total capacity of 5000 MW. Secondly, there are the Advanced Gas-cooled Reactor (AGR) stations of which two (Dungeness B and Hinkley Point B) were building in early 1969, with a third, Hunterston B, being constructed in Scotland. Another AGR station at Seaton Carew was agreed in mid-1968 and one at Heysham was started in 1970. Because of technological and constructional difficulties, all these stations, except Heysham, are well behind schedule. Thirdly, there are stations based on the Fast Breeder Reactors (FBR) which will make up the third generation of nuclear stations in the late 1970s. These are still at the prototype stage.

Nuclear stations have high capital costs relative to conventional stations. The capital cost per kilowatt of the later Magnox stations was about £125, while comparable 2000 MW coal and nuclear AGR stations would have capital costs per kW of about £65 and £95 respectively.[1] As a result of this, fuel costs are a much higher proportion of total generating costs (capital costs and running costs) in conventional stations than they are in nuclear stations: in conventional stations, fuel costs are two thirds of total generating costs compared with only one fifth in nuclear stations. Although the generating costs of nuclear stations have fallen over the past decade and the trend is expected to continue, the early Magnox stations proved to have higher generating costs than had initially been forecast. These stations were planned in the mid 1950s on the basis of several assumptions: that the maximum size of conventional stations had already been reached and further

1. Reply to Parliamentary question, 13 December 1967. Estimates of capital costs for actual stations tend to be difficult to interpret, since any comparison depends on knowing the detailed assumptions on which the estimates were based. In 1968 it was expected that the capital cost differential between coal and AGR stations would narrow still further; see Select Committee on Nationalized Industries (1968), *The Exploitation of North Sea Gas*, HMSO, p. 124. Delays with the AGR stations had, by 1972, made this very unlikely.

technological advances were unlikely; that fuel costs of conventional stations would continue to rise; that nuclear stations would cost £140–£150 per kW; and that with an interest rate of 5 per cent and allowing a credit for the plutonium which the stations produced, nuclear power would be competitive with conventional. Several of these assumptions were not borne out in practice. There were spectacular advances in thermal technology, the capital cost estimates were too low, interest rates rose to 8 per cent, and the price of plutonium fell. Consequently the total generating cost per kWh of the Magnox stations is higher than that of the most efficient coal-fired stations, even though their fuel cost is much lower. Berkeley, the first Magnox station, had generating costs of 1·27d. (0·53p) per kWh in 1967 as against an estimated cost of 0·54d. (0·23p) in 1968 for Ratcliffe, the best coal-fired station. Later Magnox stations, with their lower capital costs, are, however, generating at lower costs than the early stations. Wylfa, the last Magnox type of station, was expected to generate electricity at 0·70d. (0·29p) per kWh.

The AGR stations were expected to have lower generating costs than the Magnox stations and initially were expected to be able to beat the best coal stations. The *Fuel Policy* White Paper in 1967 forecast generating costs of 0·52d. (0·225p) for Dungeness B and 0·48d. (0·2p) for Hinkley Point B. Since then the estimates have been raised as a result of devaluation, the use of an 8 per cent discount rate in place of 7½ per cent, and the use of the same rate of interest during construction instead of 5 per cent. These factors have been partly offset by the use, since 1969, of a twenty-five-year amortization period for AGR stations instead of, as earlier, a twenty-year period. Conventional stations are assumed to have a thirty-year life. Nonetheless, the revised cost estimates for the AGR stations show an increase in estimated generating costs. In early 1969 it was estimated that Dungeness B would generate at 0·56d. (0·23p) and Hinkley Point B at 0·52d. (0·22p). Dungeness B was thus expected to generate at costs above those of the coal-fired Ratcliffe station. It was anticipated, however, that the cost of generation in the later AGR stations would decline. The 1967 White Paper foresaw that 'by about 1980, AGR generation costs should be down to a level at least 20 per cent below those of the AGR stations now under construction, and should then be fully competitive with generation from un-taxed oil'.[1] Construction and technological problems have since badly frustrated these hopes.

The third generation FBR nuclear stations are expected to reduce costs of nuclear generation considerably. Rough estimates are that their generating costs will be around 0·26d (0·11p) per kWh. However, these stations are unlikely to be in operation before 1980 and it would not be unusual if their es-timated costs rose in the meantime. The generation of elec-tricity through fusion as opposed to fission could have even lower costs than the FBRs. The technical problems of genera-tion by fusion are very great, however, and it seems unlikely that it could be used commercially before the end of the cen-tury.

Table 4 sums up the foregoing discussion by listing the actual and estimated generating costs of seven power stations using differing technologies. The reader should be warned that the cost estimates were made in early 1969 and stations coming into operation in the early 1970s may have higher actual costs than these estimates. Also, the estimates only reflect generating costs for stations of those particular sizes built at that particular time. Despite all these cautions, Table 4 is useful in that it indicates the expected competitiveness of various nuclear stations compared with the most modern con-ventional stations.

The Table does not show the cost of generating with natural gas as a fuel. The capital cost per kW of a gas-burning station would be below that of an oil or coal station[2], and total genera-ting costs with oil and gas might be roughly the same. Given the low cost of generation from oil and gas and the advances in nuclear technology as the AGR programme proceeds, it

1. *Fuel Policy*, p. 81.
2. *The Exploitation of North Sea Gas*, p. 126.

must be doubtful whether the electricity industry would, on economic grounds, choose to build any more coal-fired power stations after the completion of those being built.[1] The decision to make the Seaton Carew station a nuclear AGR station,

Table 4
Actual and Estimated Generating Costs of Power Stations

Station	Type	Output capacity MW	Commissioning date	Generating cost per kWh	
Berkeley	Magnox No. 1	275	1962	1·27d. (1967)	(0·53p)
Wylfa	Magnox No. 9	1180	1969	0·70d. (E)	(0·29p)
Dungeness B	AGR No. 1	1320	1972	0·56d. (E)	(0·23p)
Hinkley Point B	AGR No. 2	1320	1972	0·52d. (E)	(0·22p)
Ratcliffe	Coal-fired	2000	1969	0·55d. (E)	(0·23p)
Drax A	Coal-fired	1980	1971	0·61d. (E)	(0·25p)
Pembroke	Oil-fired	2000	1970	0·59d. (E) Taxed	(0·25p)
				0·48d. (E) Untaxed	(0·20p)

Notes: 1. (E) signifies estimated cost in 1968–9.
2. The Pembroke estimates show generating costs with and without the duty on oil.
3. The commissioning dates of several stations have been delayed by a variety of technical problems and their 1968–9 cost estimates are undoubtedly too low.

Source: Parliamentary Questions 1968–9; *Fuel Policy.*

1. The choice of technique is not quite as simple as this, however. Though nuclear stations have lower generating costs than conventional stations, they are very capital-intensive and capital is a scarce commodity. In some circumstances it may therefore be preferable to choose a technique which has slightly higher generating costs if it absorbs substantially less capital investment. Of course, even if it were decided for this reason to build a conventional station rather than a nuclear one, an oil-fired station may still be preferable on economic grounds to a coal station.

even though it is in the middle of the coalfields in North-East England, tends to support this view. Most of the coal-fired capacity currently being built is sited in the low-cost East Midlands and Yorkshire coalfields. In this area new capacity might be able to compete with alternative generating methods, but it appears that the industry already has sufficient generating capacity in the area and is not inclined to build it up still further. The *Fuel Policy* White Paper made the point:

The bulk of the [plant in this] area was planned in conjunction with a large north-to-south transmission capacity through the 400 kilovolt grid, and when the new stations now building are commissioned there will be sufficient generating capacity in the Midlands and South Yorkshire to load the transmission capacity fully. Further concentration of generating plant in this part of the country would require additional transmission which, in addition to its cost, would raise questions of amenity (p. 14).

The industry will of course continue to burn coal in its existing coal-fired capacity for many years to come, though the coal burn will probably fall as the older coal stations take lower merit order ratings and are used less intensively.

3. The Pricing of Electricity

We have already seen that in England and Wales the electricity industry is divided in its organization between production and marketing. The Central Electricity Generating Board has responsibility for production, the twelve Area Electricity Boards for retail distribution. In Scotland there is no such division and the two Area Boards in that region cover both production and marketing. The organizational structure in England and Wales means that there are two price or tariff structures. One is for the sale of electricity by the C.E.G.B. to the Area Boards: this 'wholesale' price is known as the bulk supply tariff. The other is for the retail sale of electricity by the Area Boards to the final consumer.

The Bulk Supply Tariff (BST) is intended to recover the cost of generating electricity sent out to the Area Boards and to provide a surplus for the C.E.G.B. To do this, the BST has a complex two-part structure, involving running charges and capacity charges.[1] The running charges are designed to cover the running costs of power stations. We have already seen how power stations are operated in merit order according to their running costs, so that base-load electricity is supplied by the lowest-cost stations. As demand on the system rises, less efficient stations are brought on load, and the marginal cost of electricity rises. Peak demand is supplied by the highest-cost stations which only operate for short periods. In order to reflect the rising running costs of generation as demand on the system increases, the BST running charges have three rates: the peak period running rate (about 250–260 hours in the year), the day running rate (about 5600 hours), and the night period running rate (about 2900 hours). The rates set by the C.E.G.B. for these three periods in 1967/8 were 1·0d (0·42p), 0·6d (0·25p) and 0·47d (0·20p) respectively. However, these rates are based on a fuel cost to the C.E.G.B. of 85s. (£4·25) per ton of coal. If the fuel cost rises above this figure, generating costs rise and the price paid by the Area Boards rises in proportion to the excess fuel cost. In 1967/8, for example, the actual prices per kWh paid by the Area Boards were 0·109d. (0·05p) higher than those set out above.

The capacity charges in the BST are designed to reflect the fixed costs of the electricity system, and there are two such charges. One, the basic capacity charge, is related to the costs incurred in providing the basic capacity of the system; the other, the peak capacity charge, is related to the costs of providing the plant capacity intended for use during peak periods only. Studies by the C.E.G.B. of the pattern of demand showed that loads on the system in excess of 90 per cent of the system maximum demand occurred relatively infrequently, for a total annual duration of about 250 hours, and the peak capacity charge is based on this finding. Peak capacity is

1. For details of the Bulk Supply Tariff, see National Board for Prices and Incomes (1968). Report no. 59, *The Bulk Supply Tariff of the C.E.G.B.*, H.M.S.O., Cmnd 3575; C.E.G.B., *Annual Report and Accounts 1965/6*, pp. 48–52; and Meek, R. L. (1968), 'The new bulk supply tariff for electricity' *Economic Journal*, vol. 78, pp. 43–66.

defined as 10 per cent of the forecast system maximum demand, and the total peak capacity charge which the C.E.G.B. collects is equal to this peak capacity (in kW's) multiplied by a charge per kW, which in 1968 was £4. The basic capacity charge is meant to cover the costs of providing the basic capacity of the system, but it is also designed 'to collect the residue of the Generating Board's total estimated costs in the year of account after deducting the sums to be collected by the Peaking Capacity Charge and the three Running Rates'.[1] The capacity charges are levied as lump sums, and in 1967/8 the peak capacity charge totalled £14·6 million and the basic capacity charge £365·4 million. These charges are allocated between the Area Boards according to their use of peak capacity and basic capacity, i.e. in proportion to their demands on the system at particular times.

The Bulk Supply Tariff 'virtually guarantees the C.E.G.B. the recovery of all its estimated costs'.[2] It also means that the Area Boards do not know in advance what charges they will bear. This is partly because fuel prices may rise, but also because of the way in which capacity charges are allocated. Though the C.E.G.B. gives the Boards a forward estimate of capacity charges, the actual amount payable can diverge from this. The Area Boards' finances are therefore much more sensitive to divergences of actual sales from estimated sales, and the economic risks lie not with the C.E.G.B. but with the Area Boards. However, the Bulk Supply Tariff is a quite sophisticated attempt to relate price to the different costs of supplying electricity at particular times, so that electricity produced at peak periods in higher-cost power stations is supplied to the Area Boards at a price which reflects these higher costs.

It is worth stressing here that in the electricity industry, as in any other industry, the price paid should as far as possible reflect the marginal cost of supply. If prices do not reflect costs, there may be cross-subsidization with some consumers paying a price below marginal cost and others paying a price above marginal cost. In electricity supply, where the marginal

1. C.E.G.B., *Annual Report and Accounts 1965/6*, pp. 50–51.
2. Prices and Incomes Board, Report no.59, p. 4.

cost of providing electricity at peak hours is much higher than that of providing electricity at off-peak times, it is obviously undesirable that peak consumers should pay a price below this marginal cost, since this would lead to an artificial stimulation of peak demand and over-investment in electricity capacity to meet peak demand. The rule that prices should accurately reflect costs is therefore necessary to prevent misallocation of resources, and this rule should be applied as far as possible at both the 'wholesale' and 'retail' level of electricity sales.

The other major part of tariff structure in electricity is the retail tariff at which the Area Boards and the Scottish Boards sell electricity to the final consumer. Since the Boards are responsible for tariffs within their own areas, rates are not uniform throughout the country, but all the Boards are subject to the same statutory obligations in fixing tariffs. These obligations require them to cheapen the supply of electricity where possible, to simplify and standardize methods of charging, and to avoid showing undue preference to any consumer or group of consumers. These requirements are not entirely compatible, as we shall see, mainly because an efficient tariff system is unlikely to be simple.

The level and structure of retail tariffs vary between types of customer. The Boards have different tariffs for domestic, industrial, commercial and farm users, and there is usually a variety of different tariff arrangements for each group, especially for domestic and industrial consumers. Domestic consumers usually pay a fixed small amount per quarter or month for rental of metering equipment. They are then subject to a two-part tariff in respect of electricity used. This may involve a high fixed standing charge, plus a single price per kWh (or unit) of electricity consumed, or it may consist of a relatively high price per unit for a specified primary block or number of units, and a lower rate for units subsequently consumed. Sometimes there are several lower rates in respect of additional blocks of units consumed, the rate per unit decreasing as consumption increases. One might regard the two parts of the domestic tariff as being equivalent to capacity and running charges, with the high standing charge or primary price per unit reflecting the cost to the industry of maintaining capacity to supply the consumer, and the lower running rates reflecting the cost of generating power and actually supplying the consumer.[1] However, the equivalence is only very rough. The fixed charge or high basic charge normally depends on the size of the consumer's premises and not on his demand on the system. Domestic tariffs therefore do not in general give a very close relationship between the price a consumer pays and the cost of supplying him with power.

The industrial tariff generally attempts to reflect capacity and running costs in a different way. Industrial users tend to be large consumers of power, and they are usually subject to a maximum demand tariff. This is a complicated type of tariff, and we can only sketch its principles here.[2] The metering devices used for industrial consumers show not only the amount of power used, as in a domestic meter, but also the maximum demand in kW which that consumer has made on the system at any period of time. Under the maximum demand tariff the industrial user pays a high fixed charge per kW of maximum demand as registered on his meter, and he then pays a charge per unit in respect of electricity actually used. This charge per unit varies depending on whether he uses electricity at the period of his maximum demand on the system, and as more units are used the price per unit falls. Under the maximum demand tariff, the fixed charge represents a more accurate estimate of capacity costs than does the primary charge under the domestic tariff, and the running charge per unit again reflects the cost of generating and supplying power.

Both the domestic and the industrial tariffs are promotional in that the average charge per unit falls as consumption of power increases, but neither tariff necessarily charges the consumer according to the actual cost of supplying him with electricity since no account is taken of the time at which the

1. Another way of looking at this is that the fixed or primary charges cover *demand-related costs* (i.e. costs which vary with the demand made on the system) and the running charge covers *unit-related costs* (i.e. costs which vary with the supply of power).

2. The details of the industrial tariffs can be found in the annual reports of the Area Boards.

consumer is using power. In the domestic market, a consumer using electricity at 5 p.m. when the total demand on the system is very high pays the same price per unit as for power taken at 3 p.m., even though the cost of supplying the former peak-hour demand is much higher. Similarly, though the maximum demand tariff ensures that the industrial consumer pays a charge in respect of his total demand on the system, this charge does not vary according to when his maximum demand occurs. Obviously, an industrial consumer whose maximum demand coincides with domestic peak demand is imposing much heavier costs on the system than one whose maximum demand occurs at an off-peak period.[1]

In fact some Area Boards have modified the tariff structure described above, especially in the domestic sector, to try to relate price more closely to the cost of supply and to induce consumption at off-peak periods. Electricity used for domestic bulk storage heaters is taken only at off-peak periods, mainly at night when the industry is using its lowest-cost plant, and is specially metered and charged at a lower rate than normal domestic consumption. In 1967/8 one Area Board introduced a system offering a lower tariff for supplies taken only at night. Several Boards charge industrial and commercial users higher tariffs for electricity used in winter and this reflects the higher cost of meeting demand in that season. In 1968/9 a new 'Day-Night' tariff was introduced, under which all electricity used in the off-peak night period is charged at a lower rate than the normal day-time rate. A special 'white meter' automatically adjusts the charge per unit for day and night consumption, thereby eliminating the need for a special off-peak circuit and meter.

All these tariff modifications are designed to encourage consumers to take electricity during off-peak periods when the demand on the system is low, and, where possible, to substitute off-peak consumption for daytime consumption, e.g. by the use of bulk storage heaters. Greater off-peak consumption

1. In practice, an industrial consumer is likely to have a fairly constant demand for electricity throughout the working day, so that his average demand and his maximum demand are much the same.

tends to improve the industry's system load factor,[1] with a better use of capacity and a reduction in capital costs per unit of output. The industry's system load factor in England and Wales rose from 47·4 per cent in 1959/60 to 52·5 per cent in 1967/8, and a major reason was the growth in off-peak consumption (especially for domestic uses). Though the industry has attempted to offer tariff concessions for off-peak use, it has in general been reluctant to penalize peak consumers by charging prices which would deter consumption at times of high demand on the system. In part this is because there is no clear evidence that higher prices would in fact deter consumption: it has been suggested that peak demand is inelastic with respect to price and that demand would only be choked off by penal rates many times higher than the normal tariff.[2] However, even though the pricing structure may not be able to alter the pattern of demand significantly, it is important that the tariff which a consumer pays for electricity should as far as possible reflect the costs incurred in providing him with that electricity.

One of the main problems for the electricity industry is therefore to develop a pricing system which relates price per unit to the cost of supply. Since the cost of electricity increases as the total system demand increases and higher-cost stations are brought on load, the ideal pricing system would be one which related price per unit to the total demand on the system at the time the electricity was taken. Power taken when the total demand on the system was low would be charged at a lower rate than power taken when the total system demand was high, and in general terms the consumer would pay a higher price insofar as his particular demand for electricity coincided with the maximum demand on the system. Unfortunately such a price structure would be very expensive to introduce because of the complicated metering devices required.

1. The system load factor is the average load on the supply system throughout the year as a percentage of the maximum load on the system in any half-hour during the year.

2. Select Committee on Nationalised Industries (1963), *The Electricity Supply Industry*, H.M.S.O., vol. 1, pp. 66–72.

It would also make the tariff system extremely difficult for the consumer to understand, since price per unit would depend not only on his own consumption but on the total system demand of which he has no knowledge. A simpler system is needed, and one possibility is to use the known patterns of demand on the system to derive a new tariff structure based on the time at which electricity is taken. It is known that total system demand is higher in winter than in summer, and higher at certain times of the day than at others, mainly because of variations in domestic demand. As far as seasonal variations are concerned, it would be possible to charge consumers a higher rate per unit in the winter period and a lower rate per unit for the rest of the year. Daily peaks cause more of a problem, and the only practicable charging system here would be to vary rates according to the time of day at which power was taken, with considerably higher tariffs during peak periods than during the rest of the day. A time-of-day tariff would be a refinement as would the development of existing off-peak charging methods, but these would suffer to some extent from the same difficulties as a maximum demand-based tariff; i.e. meters would be costly and the system would be difficult to understand.[1] A time-of-day tariff could not solve the problem of relating price to cost of supply during erratic peaks or unexpected periods of exceptionally high demand on the system, when the marginal cost of supplying electricity is higher than even the normal peak-hour cost. However, it would have the considerable advantage that the consumer, especially the domestic consumer, would pay a price which more closely reflected the cost of supplying him than does the present tariff structure.

1. For an interesting exercise in the development of a time-of-day tariff see Crew, M. (1966), *Pennine Electricity Board: A Study in Tariff Pricing*, Bradford Exercises in Management, no. 8, Nelson; also abridged in Turvey, R. (ed.) (1968), *Public Enterprise*, Penguin Books. Crew estimated that time-of-day tariffs for half the consumers would cost £225–250 million, equal to about one-third of the electricity industry's annual investment.

4. The Financial Performance of the Electricity Industry

During the five year period 1962/3 to 1966/7, the electricity industry in England and Wales was statutorily obliged to earn a gross return of 12·4 per cent on net assets.[1] The obligation was continued in 1967/8. The South of Scotland Electricity Board was given the same obligation. The North of Scotland Hydro-Electric Board was not given a target rate of return but 'as an interim measure the N.S.H.E.B. agreed to apply such tariff increases as would give a similar percentage increase in revenue as the tariff increases applied by the S.S.E.B.'.[2] The targets set for the electricity industry were the highest in the fuel sector up to 1969. However, in the period up to March 1974 both the electricity and gas industries have been given target rates of 7 per cent, net of depreciation. For the electricity industry this represents a slightly higher rate than before.

Table 5 shows the financial performance of the industry in England and Wales over the period 1962/3 to 1967/8. The electricity industry in England and Wales did not on average attain its targets over the period. The South of Scotland Electricity Board also fell short of its targets and in fact by more than the industry in England and Wales, while the North of Scotland Hydro-Electric Board had a rate of return about half that of the industry in England and Wales. The electricity industry was not alone in failing to meet its objectives. Most other nationalized industries had returns which were below the targets set.

The major reasons for the industry's failure to achieve the required rate of return were the over-optimistic estimates of demand during the 1960s and, in consequence, the excessive size of its investment programme. This meant that the industry had expanded its net assets in the expectation that the flow of income from increased sales would enable the target rate of

1. The industry's financial obligations, as well as those of other nationalized industries, are to be found in the White Paper, *Nationalized Industries: A Review of Economic and Financial Objectives* (1967), H.M.S.O., Cmnd 3437.
2. ibid., p. 16.

Table 5
Financial Performance of the Electricity Supply Industry
England and Wales

| | Year ended 31 March | | | | | |
	1963	1964	1965	1966	1967	1968
Fixed Investment (£m)	381	464	521	595	616	631
Net Assets (£m)	2561	2874	3224	3626	4026	4502
Gross Income (£m)	273	322	349	412	395	481
Balance after depreciation and interest and financial charges (£m)	43	70	64	85	21	55
Gross income as per cent of net assets	11·9	12·6	12·1	12·6	10·9	11·7

Note: Gross Income is income before interest and depreciation is charged.
Source: Electricity Council, *Annual Report and Accounts 1967/8*.

return to be met. Sales did not grow as expected, so that the industry was left with net assets which were earning less than had been anticipated. However, the forecasting of demand and planning of investment was not easy, as the experience of the industry shows. Following years of underestimating demand during the 1950s and the serious inadequacy of the industry's capacity in 1962/3 when the abnormal winter peak could not be met, it raised its demand forecasts and also decided to plan for a plant margin of 17 per cent in order to meet abnormal winter loads, rather than 14 per cent as had previously been the case. However, the industry did not expect to reach this higher margin until 1970/71. The publication of the National Plan in 1965 also led the industry to expect faster growth of the economy, industrial production and electricity demand. In fact, demand did not show the expected trends: the 1963 forecast of 1968/9 demand was 31 per cent above the 1968 forecast.[1] But since power stations take five years to build, the investment programmes are inflexible and difficult to cut. The consequence was that the industry was left with more surplus capacity than it had planned for. On the basis of estimates of

1. Prices and Incomes Board, Report no. 59, p. 8.

demand for 1968/9, the actual plant margin was 23 per cent, instead of an expected 14 per cent.

The margin of usable capacity would have been even greater had there not been considerable technical problems. These took two forms. Firstly, there were delays in the construction of power stations because of the greatly expanded investment programme and lack of capacity in the contracting and electrical plant industries. These delays resulted in the commissioning programme running about eighteen months late in 1968/9.[1] Secondly, there were technical difficulties in the initial operation of the large efficient 500 MW sets between 1966 and 1969. This meant that completed power stations took a long time to operate at full efficiency. These two problems forced the industry to use plant which was less efficient and had higher costs than the new stations, and the power stations experiencing teething troubles constituted a substantial addition to the industry's net assets but were not earning the income which had been expected of them. This contributed to the industry's failure to meet its target rate of return in 1965–8.

5. The Future of the Industry

Forecasts into the mid-1970s of demand and supply conditions of the electricity industry are extremely difficult to make. They depend on technical and commercial factors which are rapidly changing and not easily predictable, and as we have seen, past forecasts with respect both to demand and supply have often been unreliable. Estimates made in 1967 were that the industry would be meeting a maximum simultaneous demand on the system in Great Britain of 61,000 MW by 1972/3, about 50 per cent above the 1966/7 level, with domestic and industrial demand both growing by about 70 per cent.[2] By 1969 the estimates were obviously over-optimistic. No firm estimates were available for Great Britain, but estimates made for England and Wales would seem to indicate that the 1967

1. For details of this, see *Report of the Committee of Enquiry into Delays in Commissioning C.E.G.B. Power Stations* (1969), H.M.S.O., Cmnd 3960.

2. *Fuel Policy*, p. 14.

estimate of maximum system demand for 1972/3 would not be met until 1974/5. This downward revision was a result of two major factors, the continued slow growth of the economy, and the expected continuation in the growth of off-peak sales, especially for domestic space-heating. The latter meant that although the maximum system demand estimates were revised downwards, the Electricity Council took an optimistic view about over-all unit sales, and in 1969 the forecast for 1974/5 was 230,000 GWh compared with actual sales of 161,664 GWh in 1967.

The expectation of a continued high growth of unit sales (53 per cent over the seven-year period 1967/8 to 1974/5) reflected the industry's view that natural gas would not make any major inroads into its markets. In evidence to the Select Committee on North Sea Gas, the industry considered that its industrial markets were fairly secure and that growth of demand was more likely to be influenced by industrial growth than by competition from other fuels. Electricity is used in industry for heating purposes only when severe technical requirements have to be met, e.g. clean atmosphere, precise controllability, and when 'the degree of competition with other fuels is more likely to turn on the extent to which they may be able to be developed to meet these technical requirements than on reductions in price'.[1] The industry considered the domestic space and water heating market to be more vulnerable to price competition, even though 'electricity has advantages, sometimes substantial, in the cost of appliances, installation costs (absence of chimneys, etc.), efficiency of use and of cleanliness, convenience and flexibility' and 'when all the relevant factors are taken into account, electricity offers and will continue to offer a highly competitive service in the space and water heating field'.[2] The price of fuel was considered unimportant in the choice of cooker, the remaining major domestic market. Factors such as tradition, design

1. *The Exploitation of North Sea Gas*, p. 120.
2. *The Exploitation of North Sea Gas*, p. 121. It is interesting to note that the Ministry of Power witness considered that the electricity industry might be underestimating the competitive power of natural gas.

and cleanliness appear to be more important than fuel price.

On the supply side, trends which will obviously continue into the 1970s are the increased size of power stations, and the increasing proportion of nuclear capacity as the AGR programme is implemented. This will have two consequences. First, the industry will become more capital-intensive. This has already been happening, as Table 6 shows. Capital charges were estimated to account for almost two-fifths of total costs in 1968/9, and the more capital-intensive production becomes the more necessary it is to achieve high plant load factors, so as to spread capital charges over as high an output as possible.

Table 6
Pattern of Costs (C.E.G.B.): Per Cent

	1955–6	1960–61	1966–7	1968–9 (est.)
Fuel	58	53	45	41
Capital charges	22	29	34	38
Salaries	12	11	12	12
Other	8	7	9	9
	100	100	100	100

Source: National Board for Prices and Incomes (1968), Report no. 59, *The Bulk Supply Tariff of the C.E.G.B.*, HMSO, Cmnd 3575, p. 6

The second consequence will be a change in the use of fuels. Nuclear generation will increase, but it is much less clear how the consumption of other fuels will change in the future. The industry will have greater capacity for coal burning by the mid-1970s, but some of the plant will be old and relatively inefficient. Much, of course, depends on whether the coal industry can fulfil its productivity and cost objectives, and deliver coal to the electricity industry at 4d. (1·67p) per therm or less[1]. But the use of coal also depends on the extent to which the political pressures to protect coal continue, showing

1. In 1966/7 only about fourteen million tons of coal taken by the electricity industry had a delivered cost of 4d. (1·67p) per therm or less. This was less than one-quarter of the industry's coal consumption in that year; see *The Exploitation of North Sea Gas*, p. 114.

themselves either by a continued limitation on the electricity industry in its fuel choice for new stations, or through a requirement of the industry to consume a specified amount above what would be its burn on commercial grounds, with subsequent compensation for this by the Government. Under the Coal Industry Act 1967 the electricity industry received compensation for using six million tons of coal per annum more than it would use on economic grounds. In 1970, the Conservative Government decided to end the subsidy for extra coal burnt as from mid-1971. This was a period when coal was in short supply. In December 1972, however, plans were announced to reintroduce a similar system.

A fairly safe forecast on the supply side was that station thermal efficiencies would rise. In the late 1960s the industry was experiencing serious technical problems with its new 500 M W sets so that these theoretically highly efficient sets were used less intensively than expected. The problems with these sets were resolved more slowly than expected and, combined with other factors, this adversely affected the industry's financial performance between 1969/70 and 1970/71.

It will be recalled that the industry in England and Wales was set a target net return of 7 per cent of average net assets for the quinquennium of 1969/70-1973/4. Its performance in 1968/9 augured well for the quinquennium. It made an operating profit of £323 million before interest (equal to a net return of 7·1 per cent) and a profit after interest of £101 million. This outcome was such that the industry felt able to make a slight price reduction for industrial users. In the event the three years 1969/70 to 1971/2 saw net returns of 6·4, 4·1 and 5·1 per cent respectively. In 1970/71 it made a loss after interest of £56 million, its first since nationalization, and a further loss of £23 million in 1971/2. The Electricity Council's Annual Report for 1971/2 noted that the cumulative net return for the first three years of the quinquennium was only 5·2 per cent, representing a shortfall of £269 million which had to be made up if the quinquennium target was to be achieved. The Report commented that 'achievement of the objective for the quinquennium was virtually impossible.'

The industry's poor financial performance was a consequence of several factors. First, growth of demand was slow, rising from 168,230 GWh in 1969/70 to 177,679 GWh in 1971/2, an annual growth rate of only 2·8 per cent. This slow growth was largely a result of a depressed national economy. Industrial demand was particularly sluggish, falling from 70,785 GWh in 1969/70 to 70,500 GWh in 1971/2, though this was partly due to the effects of the 1972 coal strike. Secondly, the industry was hit by a number of technological problems. The AGR stations experienced serious construction delays, the Magnox stations suffered what seem to be permanent corrosion problems and had to be run below design temperatures and output while the new big 500 MW sets, ran into boiler and turbine problems. These problems inflicted repair and modification costs upon the industry and, probably more important, meant that the industry had to run its less efficient plant more intensively to make up for the lost capacity. Thirdly, the coal strike in early 1972 affected the industry's 1971/2 performance. Fuel supplies to power stations were picketed and stations had to be used according to fuel availability rather than the merit order system. Eventually, fuel supplies became so low that electricity output had to be cut back. The slow growth of demand 1969/72 in part reflects this. Fourthly, there were very large increases in oil and coal prices during the late 1960s and early 1970s. Between 1968/9 and 1971/2 prices rose by 45 per cent. Finally, and most important, the industry was able to recoup only a small proportion of its rising costs through price increases since, at the Government's request, it had limited its price rises. In its 1971/72 Annual Report the Electricity Council estimated that 'since the Government intervened in the pricing field in the autumn of 1970, the additional revenue which Boards would have raised but for this constraint amounted to about £165 million.' In 1972 the Council was arguing that the industry should be compensated for its adherence to the price restraint policy.

The coal strike and associated picketing of power stations had a traumatic effect on the electricity industry and appears to have made it even more determined to cut its dependence on coal. The CEGB's Annual Report for 1971/2 made this clear. 'Oil-fired and nuclear stations have shared, and will continue to share, the new generating capacity on the system.' The Board admitted that oil prices will probably rise but 'ultimately, however, the hedge against excessive oil prices must be nuclear power and not coal.' It was clear that the Board would like to convert more of its existing capacity away from coal and at least towards dual firing.

Although the industry sees nuclear stations playing a bigger role in electricity generation, there are some major question marks about which nuclear system should be used. Most people have few doubts that the FBRs will be a vital component but not before 1980. Another nuclear system is needed in the meantime, not least to supply plutonium by-products to fuel the FBRs. In the late 1960s it was hoped that the AGRs would fill this gap but, as we have seen, these ran into considerable problems. In 1970 the Vinter Committee was set up to advise on future nuclear systems and reported in mid 1972. It was agreed to organize and amalgamate the nuclear power plant industry and to push ahead rapidly with FBR development. The Committee, however, was unable to make any firm decision on other components of the future nuclear system and the problem was passed to a newly created Nuclear Power Board, expected to report at the end of 1973. The position in respect of likely nuclear systems for the future is now as confused as it has ever been.

3 The Gas Industry

Few industries, nationalized or otherwise, have experienced so rapid a change of fortune as the gas industry. Up to 1960 demand for the industry's product was hardly growing at all and its share of the energy market was falling, but during the 1960s it modernized both production techniques and the 'image' of gas as a fuel. The discovery of natural gas in the North Sea has given promise of a new low-price form of energy and has assured the gas industry of continued growth throughout the 1970s, albeit with radical changes in its structure and economic policies. The present and future developments are best understood in the context of the gas industry as it was in 1960, and section 1 outlines the problems which the industry faced at the beginning of the decade. Section 2 takes up the story during the 1960s and shows how changing technology gave hopes of a more efficient and prosperous gas industry, while the remaining sections deal with the discovery, exploitation and pricing of natural gas, and with its likely future effects on the industry.

1. The Traditional Gas Industry

Before the Second World War the gas industry consisted of hundreds of undertakings operating under statutory control, mostly small producers serving a limited geographical area. One of the main reasons for nationalization was that average size of plant was well below the economic optimum, and only a co-ordinated plan could change the structure of the industry and make it more efficient. The Gas Act 1948 which nationalized the industry, set up twelve Area Boards with power to manufacture, buy and distribute gas in their areas, and the Gas Council, which acted as co-ordinator and supervisor of the Boards' activities with responsibility for the raising of capital, for industrial relations and research. The industry was quite highly decentralized in that the Boards had full control of their own production, investment, pricing and marketing policies. There was no national system for the distribution of gas, and inter-Board transfers of gas were almost non-existent. This lack of a national distribution 'grid' was of little consequence before 1960, since the production of gas in very large plants supplying the demands of a number of Boards seemed to be technically and economically impossible.

Gas was made by three different processes:

1. *Carbonization:* this involved heating certain types of coal in closed vessels. In addition to coal gas, this process produced a number of by-products, especially coke, and the economics of the process depended on the sale of these by-products.

2. *Water gas:* steam and air were blown through hot coke and gave a 'lean' gas of low calorific value which had to be enriched to bring it up to the standards required for distribution.[1]

3. *Oil gas:* various processes existed in which oil was decomposed by heat to give gas.

As well as manufacturing gas, all Boards bought some gas, mainly from the Coal Board or the steel industry which operated coke ovens to manufacture coke and produced gas as a by-product. Coke oven gas was particularly important in Wales, the East Midlands and the Northern region. Another source of bought gas was methane from coal mines, and a very small amount of domestic natural gas was exploited by two Area Boards. Table 7 shows the proportions of each type of gas supplied.

Between 1950/51 and 1959/60 sales of gas rose by only 5 per cent in total. Increases in industrial and commercial

1. The calorific value is the heat output of a given quantity of gas. The standard measure of heat output is the British Thermal Unit (Btu), and the gas industry measures its output either in cubic feet, or in therms. One therm is equal to 100,000 Btu's.

Table 7
Gas Supplied (as Per Cent of Total Available)

| | Gas made | | | | Gas bought | | |
	Coal	Water	Oil	Other	Total	Coke ovens	Other	Total
1950/51	71	15	—	1·9	87·9	12	0·3	12·3
1959/60	61	14	2·2	0·9	78·2	17	4·5	21·5

Note: The 1959/60 totals do not add, presumably because of rounding.

Source: Select Committee on Nationalised Industries (1961), *The Gas Industry*, H.M.S.O., vol. 1, p. 63.

sales were offset by a decline in domestic sales which were almost half of total sales in 1959/60. In the same period, electricity sales increased by about 125 per cent and oil sales by 145 per cent, so that the share of gas in total fuel consumption declined from $17\frac{1}{2}$ per cent to 14 per cent. The sluggish growth of gas sales partly reflects the rapid increase in gas prices between 1950 and 1960 relative to those of competing fuels, 64 per cent as against 24 per cent for electricity and 40 per cent for oil, and this rise in gas prices in turn reflects the pattern of costs in the industry. In 1959/60, 61 per cent of gas-making capacity was based on the carbonization of coal, and there were several reasons why this technique tended to mean that costs and prices were higher and likely to rise faster than those of competing fuels. Firstly, the high-grade coal from which gas could be obtained was relatively scarce and difficult to mine, and it also required substantial preparation at the pithead. It therefore cost more than the low-grade coal used by the electricity industry, and because it was becoming progressively scarcer, the price of gas coal rose by 70 per cent between 1951 and 1960 compared with only 45 per cent for the price of coal to the electricity industry. All indications were that the relative price of gas coal would continue to increase. Secondly, the carbonization process had high capital and running costs and could only operate economically with a high load factor and preferably producing continuously.[1] This meant that carbonization plants could not be used to meet seasonal or daily peaks, and while the industry could store gas to meet daily peaks, it could not even out fluctuations in summer/winter production so as to allow carbonization plants to produce continuously. Thirdly, even with a favourable load factor, carbonization plants were a very expensive way of making gas, as Table 8 shows.

It was much cheaper to buy gas than make it from coal, but the supply of bought gas was outside the industry's

Table 8
Cost of Production of Gas 1959/60

Made gas	Pence per therm
Coal gas	12d (5p)–15d (6·25p) assuming high load factor
Water gas	9·6d (4p)–15d (6·25p) depending on technique and load factor
Oil gas	8·2d (3·42p)–10d (4·17p) with favourable load factor 12·8d (5·33p) used for peak load

Bought gas	Pence per therm
Coke ovens	6·5d (2·71p), before purifying
Refinery gas	8d (3·32p)–8·9d (3·71p)
Mine methane	5·5d (2·9p), before purifying
Domestic natural gas	7·2d (3p)–8·3d (3·46p)

Source: *The Gas Industry*, vol. 1, p. 72.

own control, and only 21·5 per cent of total gas available in 1959/60 was bought. Water gas and oil gas were relatively inexpensive ways of producing small amounts of gas to meet peak demands, but the carbonization process was the only one

1. The load factor of a plant is the actual amount of gas produced in a given time as a percentage of the maximum amount it could have produced in that time.

which could produce gas in the volumes needed by the industry.

The problems of the industry in 1959/60 were therefore that demand was stagnant, prices were rising relative to competitive fuels, and the bulk of output came from a high-cost production method based on coal whose price was continuing to rise. The Gas Council was at that time anxious to find a technique which would produce gas at a cost of 8d. (3·3p)– 8½d. (3·5p) per therm, but none of the techniques then operating could do this.

2. The Gas Industry 1960–67

In the early 1960s, there were three potential sources of cheaper gas.

1. *The Lurgi process:* this used low-grade cheaper coal and gasified it completely, without producing coke as a by-product. The process had been extensively discussed during the 1950s, and two plants of 30 mcfd and 40 mcfd respectively were constructed and came into commission in the early 1960s.[1] These produced gas at 9·64d. (4·02p) and 11·25d. (4·69p) per therm, though costs would have been higher had not the National Coal Board supplied coal at specially low prices. However, these plants were well below the most economic size for the Lurgi process, and a large-scale study by the Gas Council and the Coal Board, which was completed in 1964, estimated that a 100 mcfd Lurgi plant could produce gas at 8¼d. (3·44p)–8½d. (3·54p) per therm given favourable load factors.

2. *Importation of methane:* after extensive trials, the importation of liquefied methane from the natural gas fields of Algeria began in 1964. The methane was stored in refrigerated tanks at the Canvey Island terminal, and distributed through a special high-pressure gas grid to seven English Area Boards. The methane, a rich gas of high calorific value, was reformed or used to enrich lean gas (e.g. Lurgi gas), and it was estimated to cost 8½d. (3·54p)–8¾d. (3·65p) per therm.

1. mcfd = millions of cubic feet per day. This is the most common way of expressing flows by volume.

3. *Oil-gasification:* developments in this technique were much the most important change in technology. In 1962, Imperial Chemical Industries, in pursuit of a cheaper source of ammonia for fertilizer manufacture, developed a method of high-pressure steam reforming of light distillate (naphtha), and this turned out to be an extremely cheap source of lean gas. The Gas Council's engineers devised a method of enriching this gas to produce town gas.

The oil-gasification process had enormous advantages over existing or proposed coal-based methods. The capital costs were at most one-third those of a comparable Lurgi plant; plants could be scaled down to relatively small sizes without significantly affecting their economics; their production costs were much less sensitive to load factor – a drop in load factor from 87 per cent to 50 per cent would increase cost per therm by only $\frac{1}{2}$d. ($0\cdot21$p) compared with more than 2d. ($0\cdot83$p) for a Lurgi plant – and so they were flexible enough to be used on peak loads; they used much less land and labour than Lurgi plants; and they had no effluent problems. As a result, their over-all cost of production (about 7d. ($2\cdot92$p)–8d. ($3\cdot33$p) per therm) was below the most optimistic Lurgi estimate. A further substantial advantage was that the gas was produced at high pressure, which reduced the cost of transmission and made intra-Area high-pressure distribution systems possible. This enabled Boards to reduce the number of gas works.

It is hardly surprising, then, that the Gas Council decided not to proceed with the Lurgi process and Boards began to invest in oil-gasification plants. Table 9 shows maximum daily plant capacity in March 1961 and March 1968. The swing to oil gasification plants was quite spectacular, and by 1967/8 almost three-quarters of total gas-making capacity used this technique, compared with only 6·7 per cent in 1960/61. A large amount of carbonization capacity had been scrapped, and the number of gas works almost halved. One consequence of the change in production methods was a substantial shift in the raw materials used by the industry. Purchases of coal for gas making fell from over 22 million tons in 1960/61 to about 13 million tons in 1967/8, while over the same period

Table 9
Maximum Daily Plant Capacity: March 1961 and March 1968

	Millions of cu. ft. per day 1961	1968	Per cent change 1961-8	Per cent of total plant 1968
Carbonization	1341·2	646·6	−52	11·2
Lurgi	15·0	96·0	540	1·7
Oil gasification	167·3	4202·3	2412	73·1
Water gas etc.	975·8	806·8	−17	14·0
Total plant	2499·3	5751·7	130	100·0
No. of gas works	378	192	−49	—

Source: Gas Council, *Annual Reports*.

purchases of light oil rose from 0·4 million tons to 4·3 million tons.

Table 9 also shows that the maximum daily plant capacity more than doubled, and this was a result of a very large growth in the demand for gas during the 1960s. Table 10 gives details of gas sales in 1960/61 and 1967/8.

Table 10
Gas Sales 1960/61 and 1967/8

	Million therms 1960/61	1967/8	Per cent change 1960/61 to 1967/8	Per cent of total gas sold 1967/8
Domestic	1291·2	2652·1	105	63·1
Industrial	851·8	914·5	7	21·8
Commercial	405·9	569·9	40	13·6
Other	63·4	62·6	−1	1·5
Total sales	2612·3	4199·1	61	100·0

Source: Gas Council, *Annual Reports*.

In contrast to the period 1950–60 when total sales of gas increased by only 5 per cent, between 1960/61 and 1967/8 total sales increased by 61 per cent, almost entirely because of the doubling of sales in the domestic market. The success of gas in the domestic market was due largely to the promotion of the fuel in space heating. Sales of gas-space-heaters in 1967/8 were 878,998 compared with 265,258 in 1960/61, while warm-air boilers and central heating units showed an even more rapid growth. These trends in appliance sales owed much to the radical design and styling changes in gas fires and heaters, and also to the remarkably successful 'High Speed Gas' advertising campaign. This began in 1962/3 with the intention of modernizing the image of gas as a domestic fuel, and the sales data are some indication of its success.

However, the higher sales of gas to the domestic market were not an unmixed blessing. Demand for gas as a space-heating fuel tends to give rise to peak periods, and peak demand increased faster than total demand. In consequence, the proportion of gas supplied in the six winter months (October to March) rose from 57 per cent in 1960/61 to 63 per cent in 1966/7. The industry was much better able to meet these peaks than it had been in the 1950s. Oil-gasification plants had not only stabilized the net cost of gas production: they were also economic at relatively low load factors and could meet peak demand more efficiently than carbonization plants. Although the remaining carbonization plants had higher costs of production than oil-gasification plants, they were most economic when run at high load factors. They were therefore used much more intensively than oil-gasification plants, and supplied base-load gas. In 1967/8 carbonization plants supplied 34 per cent of all gas made, though they represented only 11 per cent of the industry's plant capacity.

The growth in demand for gas up to 1967/8 came largely from an increase in average consumption per user rather than an increase in the number of consumers, and the rising consumption was encouraged by the promotional tariffs charged for domestic space-heating supplies. These were two-part tariffs with an initial high fixed charge (or a high tariff per therm for the initial therms) and a lower running charge per therm for additional gas used. This running charge was below the normal tariff for general domestic use, so that the more gas a consumer used under the domestic space-heating tariff, the lower was the average price per therm. These promotional tariffs had an adverse effect on the industry's financial situation, for as more gas was sold at the lower space-heating running charge, so the overall average revenue per therm fell. In general terms, revenue per therm rose by proportionately less than sales, and despite tariff increases, income per therm hardly rose at all between 1960/61 and 1967/8 while total cost per therm increased. Table 11 shows some aspects of the industry's financial performance between 1962/3 and 1967/8.

The Gas Council's financial objective up to March 1969 was to earn a rate of return of 10·2 per cent on net assets and in the quinquennium up to 1966/7 it nearly succeeded, the average being 9·8 per cent. However, in 1967/8, a number of adverse circumstances badly affected the industry's finances. One was the effect of the Government price freeze imposed in 1966 and 1967, which meant that revenue did not rise to cover increased costs. The most important cost increases were devaluation and the oil surcharge after the 1967 Middle East war, both of which increased the cost of the imported oil feedstock. A further longer-term problem came from the investment in new developments. As the Gas Council *Annual Report* 1966/7 pointed out, this 'leads in the short run to higher costs (mainly interest and other pre-operational costs) which are creating transitional burdens larger than can be accommodated by the buoyancy of revenue achieved through expanding sales'.[1] (p. 19). The most important of these new developments, which began to be reflected in the industry's operations in 1966/7, was the discovery of natural gas beneath the North Sea. Some of the industry's problems in planning the exploitation of natural gas are directly related to the rapid growth of demand in the 1960s, but it is important to remember that in oil-gasification the industry had a low-cost technique which would have allowed it to expand its share of the fuel market even in the absence of natural gas.

1. Gas Council, *Annual Report 1966/7*, p.19.

Table 11
Investment, Income, and Return on Net Assets

Year end-ed 31 Mar	Income per therm (pence)	Expenditure per therm (pence)	Net assets (£ million)	Gross income (£ million)*	Gross income as per cent of net assets	Fixed investment (£ million)
1963	22·47 (9·36p)	22·66 (9·44p)	680	63·3	9·3	59·2
1964	22·77 (9·49p)	22·0 (9·17p)	727	72·8	10·0	92·0
1965	22·61 (9·42p)	21·58 (8·99p)	787	84·8	10·8	89·6
1966	22·47 (9·36p)	21·71 (9·05p)	851	84·8	10·0	119·0
1967	22·74 (9·48p)	22·50 (9·38p)	963	87·8	9·1	215·0
1968	22·42 (9·34p)	23·15 (9·65p)	1117	86·0	7·7	282·0

*Note: Gross income is trading surplus and other income before depreciation, taxation and interest.
Source: Gas Council, *Annual Reports*.

3. The Discovery of Natural Gas

In 1959 a very large natural gas field was discovered at Groningen in northern Holland, and this reinforced the belief of many geologists that gas-bearing rock strata also existed under the North Sea. Initially the Gas Council was interested in importing Dutch natural gas either in liquid form or by pipeline, but by 1964 the legal framework had been laid for under-sea exploration. The countries bordering the North Sea agreed on areas of exploration, and the Continental Shelf Act 1964 established the method of exploitation in the British sector. This involved a system of licensing rather than direct State participation in drilling and exploration. Interested companies or groups applied for concessions in blocks of about 100 square miles, and exclusive rights to explore were given, in the first instance for six years. However, the State retained the right to any resources found, and the Continental Shelf Act laid down that all gas had to be offered to the gas industry unless it was to be used for purposes other than that of fuel, e.g. as feedstock in the chemical industry. The Gas Act 1965 gave the Gas Council new powers 'to manufacture gas, to get or acquire gas in or from Great Britain or elsewhere and to supply gas in bulk to any Area Board', thus enabling it to act for the gas industry in negotiations for the purchase of North Sea gas from the prospecting companies.

A number of groups obtained licences to drill for gas. These were mainly oil companies acting alone or in partnership, and their experience and expertise were such that exploration and drilling proceeded at a much more rapid rate than if the the State itself had undertaken the task. In 1965 the first commercial strike had been made, and by the end of 1968 four separate large gas fields had been discovered, lying between fifteen and fifty-five miles off the coast of Eastern England. The proven reserves of gas were estimated at over 25 million million cubic feet, sufficient to give a flow of 3500 mcfd over a period of twenty to twenty-five years. The major problem for the Gas Council is to plan the exploitation of this new fuel source. The Government's fuel policy envisages the build-up of gas absorption to 2000 mcfd in 1971/2 and 4000 mcfd in the mid-1970s.[1] We shall discuss the problems of exploitation in the next section, but it should be noted that the proven reserves at the beginning of 1969 were not sufficient to provide as much gas as the mid-1970s target requires. At an absorption rate of 4000 mcfd, the present reserves would be adequate for only seventeen years' supply, so that the Government's fuel policy target for the mid-1970s assumes that more gas will be found. This is not unreasonable. In the United States, for example, proven reserves are about seventeen times present annual consumption but new reserves are continually being discovered. Also, in the North Sea search the proportion of successful wells was much higher than is customary in gas exploration, though no one can predict whether this favourable situation will continue. It is in the

1. *Fuel Policy*, p.63.

context of the need to find more gas that the price of gas to the exploring companies is important.

Under the Continental Shelf Act, all gas to be used as fuel has to be offered to the gas industry, and a price had to be negotiated between the sellers and the Gas Council as buyer. Only if the Council were thought to be refusing a reasonable price could the Minister of Power enter as arbiter. There was a considerable incentive for the Gas Council to hold out for a low price, since the rapid build-up of supplies meant that the industry would have to pursue a very aggressive marketing policy to sell the gas, and a low price per therm would give scope for reductions in retail prices. The exploring companies too were more willing to settle for a low price than if there had been a slow build-up of supplies. A slow rate of exploitation, rationing the gas out over a very long period, would have induced the companies to demand a higher price per therm to maintain the present value of their total receipts from the sale of the gas.[1] Both sides were therefore willing to settle for a 'low' price, but they had different views on what that price should be.

The initial price negotiated by the Gas Council (with B.P.) was 5d. (2·08p) per therm, but this was a short-term contract for a small amount of gas, and negotiations over the basic price for the long-term contracts were long and hard. It seems likely that the companies were initially asking for a price of 4d. (1·67p) per therm or above, while the Gas Council's first offer was probably about 2d. (0·83p) per therm. Certainly the final negotiated price of 2·87d. (1·20p) per therm was much closer to the Gas Council's original offer than to the companies' demands, and the question is whether the price is sufficiently

1. The present value of an income stream involves adding up each year's receipts after applying to each an appropriate discount factor to reflect the fact that income can be invested to earn more income. Thus the further into the future is a given sum received, the less is its value at present, simply because more investment income is foregone. In the case of the gas purchase, the exploring companies were willing to settle for a relatively low price so long as revenue built up quickly, but to secure the same present value over a longer period of years would have required a larger amount of income per annum, i.e. a higher price per therm.

high to stimulate further exploration for gas in the British sector of the North Sea. The Gas Council's view would be that the companies will make a highly satisfactory rate of return on money already spent, and that future finds can be the subject of further price negotiations. On the other hand, the companies would claim that future discoveries will be more costly to make and exploit than the initial strikes, since they were made in the most promising locations.[1] They may feel that the price negotiated for the present gas supplies does not give a rate of return high enough to warrant committing large amounts of capital to further exploration when more profitable investment opportunities exist elsewhere in the companies' operations.

It is impossible to say which of these views is correct. In 1970 about 75 per cent of the blocks licensed in 1964 were surrendered, considerably more than the legal maximum, but the retained blocks were presumably the most promising. Also, exploration efforts have moved into northern waters and it is known that gas reserves have been found in association with the oil discoveries. There is no firm evidence that the incentive to explore is too low.

However, the Gas Council and the exploring companies did agree on the price and supply conditions in respect of natural gas from the four original fields. Under these contracts the Gas Council has agreed to take an annual quantity of gas which amounts on average to 60 per cent of the installed capacity of the pipelines from the gas fields, i.e. the contract supply is based on a load factor of 60 per cent. The actual amount taken can vary within specified limits and will normally be higher in winter than in summer: this is in accordance with the seasonal pattern of gas consumption, and will also allow plant and pipeline maintenance in the summer. However, the important point is that the Gas Council has contracted to take an annual quantity based on a

1. A contrary view might be that increased geological knowledge will reduce uncertainty and lower the cost of future discoveries, but it is very difficult to predict where gas will be found and in what quantities without actually drilling for it.

60 per cent load factor, and it must pay for this quantity whether or not it takes the gas. Once the annual contract quantity has been taken additional supplies of gas are available at a lower price of 2·025d. (0·84p) per therm, but the industry has a 'minimum bill' to pay in respect of the annual contract quantity. This makes the industry's task quite clear. The Gas Council and the Area Boards must attempt to sell to consumers at least as much gas as they have contracted to take from the North Sea fields.

4. The Exploitation of Natural Gas

There are certain technical problems associated with the exploitation of natural gas. North Sea gas is mainly methane and has a calorific value twice that of manufactured town gas, i.e. a given volume gives twice as much heat. Also, North Sea gas has different combustion characteristics from town gas, and an appliance suitable for burning town gas is not suitable for burning natural gas directly. The Gas Council therefore had to decide whether to reform (or dilute) the natural gas so that it could be used in existing appliances (as had been done with most Algerian natural gas), or to convert appliances to burn natural gas. The cost of converting all 13 million consumers over the ten year period to 1978/9 is estimated to be £400 million, but the Gas Council calculated that conversion was far more economic than non-conversion.[1] Conversion of appliances will avoid the need for new expensive reforming plant, and a further enormous advantage of using natural gas direct is its effect on the distributive network. Because natural gas gives twice as many therms per cubic foot as town gas, the capacity of the distribution mains and storage system is effectively doubled when natural gas replaces town gas. However, because conversion will be carried

1. According to the Government's *Fuel Policy* White Paper, the present value of the saving by converting rather than reforming totals £1,400 million over a thirty-year period (p. 8).

out on a piecemeal basis, and because natural gas and town gas cannot share the same pipeline, a new national distribution system is required to carry the gas from the two landing points on the East Coast to the Area Boards who are in charge of local distribution. The Gas Council is constructing a high-pressure bulk transmission pipeline, which will be linked with the pipeline originally built to carry Algerian natural gas. This is a very expensive business, and it is estimated that investment in bulk transmission and storage from 1968/9 to 1972/3 will amount to £546 million compared with £177 million in the previous four-year period.

A major problem in exploiting natural gas is the question of who to sell it to, and at what price. The Government's fuel policy statements identify three types of market for gas as a fuel:

1. *The premium market:* gas has certain inherent advantages over other fuels in that it is clean, controllable and requires no storage. The premium market consists of those consumers who have shown that they value these advantages, and who are willing to pay a premium for the use of gas over and above what they would pay for an equivalent amount of heat from another fuel. The premium market is in fact the existing gas market, thirteen million domestic and 80,000 industrial users.

2. *The semi-premium market:* these consumers would be willing to pay some premium for the use of gas, but do not consider that the advantages of gas are sufficient to offset the price difference between gas and competing fuels. If the price of gas were lower these users would switch to gas, and since gas has some inherent advantage for them, they would use gas even if the price per therm were somewhat higher than that of competing fuels.

3. *The bulk market:* here any fuel is used only to provide crude heat (e.g. for firing boilers), and the determining factor in the choice of fuel is price per therm. While gas might have some slight advantage in that it does not require storage, it would be required to compete with coal and oil mainly on price alone.

It has been suggested by some economists that the allocation of natural gas should be determined by some kind of
market mechanism, i.e. that the gas should be sold first to those
consumers who are willing to pay most for it.[1] There could
be technical problems in doing this – natural gas and town gas
could not be economically supplied in the same area – but
a much more important objection is that this would not
necessarily be the most economic method of exploitation
from the national point of view.

The Government has taken the view that neither the price
nor the allocation of natural gas should be left to 'the market
mechanism'. Instead the policy is that natural gas should be
supplied first to the premium markets on the grounds that
this would give the greatest saving of real resources. The concept of total resource savings is fundamental to the Government's fuel policy. The intention is to exploit natural gas in
such a way that the total saving of resources to the economy
will be maximized. The Ministry of Power explains:

the true costs to the community of supplying the nation with the
energy it needs is measured by the value of the resources employed –
manpower, capital, material and foreign exchange. In their work on
fuel policy the Ministry have been concerned to compare the
possible alternative developments by reference to their relative
costs in resource use.[2]

Using this concept, the Ministry has calculated that 'the
greatest overall gain would be obtained by the rapid introduction of natural gas, concentrating particularly on premium
markets.'[3] But the rate of introduction is so rapid that supplies
of gas will build up too quickly for the premium market to

---

1. See, for example, Polanyi, G. (1967), *What Price North Sea Gas?*,
Hobart Paper no. 38, Institute of Economic Affairs.
2. *The Exploitation of North Sea Gas*, p.194.
3. *The Exploitation of North Sea Gas*, p.196. A particular gain from
supplying the premium markets first is that it will save imported oil which
would otherwise have been used to make town gas. Natural gas will
have some foreign exchange cost, since some of the supplying companies
are foreign oil companies, but the direct saving to the balance of payments will be considerable.

absorb it all, and by 1972/3 some gas will go to the non-premium markets, and some will be reformed and sold as town gas in unconverted areas. Table 12 gives estimates of gas sales for 1972/3 and 1975, compared with 1966/7.

Table 12
The Markets for Gas

| | 1966/7 | | 1972/3 | | 1975 | |
	m. therms	%	m. therms	%	m. therms	%
Domestic	2268	60	4550	51	5100	39
Industrial	908	24	3500	40	7200	54
of which						
Power stations	n.a.		n.a.		(3400	26)
Commercial etc.	599	16	825	9	1000	7
Total sales	3775	100	8875	100	13,300	100

Notes: 1. Industrial sales include both premium and bulk sales.
2. A small amount of gas was sold to power stations in 1966/7, and the 1971 estimate is 500 million therms.

Sources: 1966/7–Gas Council, *Annual Report*.
1972/3–National Board for Prices and Incomes (1969), Report no. 102, *Gas Prices* (*Second Report*), H.M.S.O., Cmnd 3974, p. 60.
1975–*Fuel Policy* White Paper, Cmnd 3438, p. 64.

The 1975 estimates are much more conjectural than those for 1972/3. They are based on specific assumptions about the rate of absorption and the proportion of gas going to power stations, and they may well understate the growth of the domestic and premium industrial markets. However, they do illustrate the point that the absorption of 4000 mcfd in 1975, equivalent to 13,000 million therms, will require considerable sales to the non-premium industrial market.

The Government's exploitation policy for natural gas is a complex of interlinked factors, and it may be useful to summarize them here. Firstly, maximum resource savings will accrue from a fast depletion rate and a concentration on the premium markets. Secondly, the fast depletion rate has allowed a lower price to be negotiated with the exploring companies. Thirdly, to reserve the gas only for the premium markets is uneconomic since the growth of these markets is insufficient to absorb the gas which the fast depletion rate is making available. Also, the distribution system would be working well below capacity if only the premium market were supplied (i.e. the system load factor would be low), and this would raise the cost of gas. Fourthly, to justify the fast depletion rate and to sell the gas which it has contracted to buy, the industry must sell to the non-premium markets where gas has little or no inherent advantage but where the main concern is to obtain low-cost crude heat. Fifthly, the low price per therm negotiated with the exploring companies makes it possible for the industry to quote prices competitive with those of oil and coal in the non-premium markets.

This discussion has been concerned with the period up to the mid-1970s and the initial stages of the exploitation of natural gas, but the use of the bulk market to balance supply and demand will continue, though at a diminished rate, when the gas is flowing at its 'plateau' rate of 4000 mcfd after 1975. After 1975 one would expect non-premium sales to bulk users to decline as premium market demand continues to rise and as supplies are diverted to the premium market in order to maximize resource savings. However, there will still be a large volume of bulk sales, and this will also be used to help ameliorate the industry's short-term problems of balancing supply and demand. We have already noted that the gas industry has daily and seasonal peaks in demand, and that the increased demand for gas as a space-heating medium has exacerbated the seasonal peak problem. This has meant a fall in the system load factor, which is the average weekly amount of gas supplied as a percentage of the amount supplied in the peak week during the winter. The advantage of premium or bulk industrial sales is that they tend to improve the system load factor, since industrial usage does not usually vary seasonally and a steady level of industrial sales increases the amount supplied in the average week by proportionately more than the amount supplied in the peak week. Thus, for example, a fifteen-year contract signed in mid-1969 between the Gas Council and I.C.I. provides for a supply by 1972 of 900 million therms per annum, an amount almost equal to the whole of 1967/8 industrial consumption, and it is estimated that this sale alone will improve the industry's system load factor by 3 percentage points. But domestic demand for space heating will continue to expand rapidly and the peak problem will continue to exist.

The advent of natural gas means that the industry will no longer need to have manufacturing plant available to meet seasonal peaks, but the exploitation of the North Sea reserves creates another difficulty. The industry has contracted to accept North Sea gas at a particular rate of flow, and though the agreed offtake of gas from the North Sea wells is higher in the winter than in the summer, the industry cannot tailor its offtake of gas exactly to the pattern of demand. Thus during the winter peaks the planned offtake rate is likely to be insufficient, while during the summer more gas may be available to the industry than a very low summer demand warrants. The obvious way of dealing with these imbalances is to store any excess summer gas and draw on it during the winter, and we shall deal with this in the next paragraph. There is, however, another way of coping with seasonal imbalances between supply and demand. A proportion of gas can be sold to non-premium users on an 'interruptible' basis. This might mean some bulk users burning natural gas in the summer and switching to other fuels (notably oil) during the winter peaks. The use of interruptible supplies might appear to be inefficient, but apparently it is relatively cheap to convert boilers to dual fuel use and would cost very little extra to design and construct boilers in this way.[1] Provided natural gas could be made available at a suitable price, some

---

1. The electricity industry estimated that it would cost £1–2 per kilowatt of capacity to convert a power station to dual fuel use (*The Exploitation of North Sea Gas*, pp. 123–4), and another witness commented that the switchover from one fuel to another 'is done in a matter of minutes' (p. 148).

bulk users might be willing to take interruptible supplies. The main result is that more gas can be sold and the contract quantity reached, but interruptible supplies also help the industry to balance out seasonal fluctuations without constructing storage facilities.

In spite of these possibilities of varying offtake rates and using interruptible supplies, the gas industry will still need storage facilities to cope with seasonal or daily peaks or with sharp unexpected increases in demand at particular times. Several methods of storage exist. One possibility is that gas could be stored in natural or man-made underground cavities or in aquifers,[1] but to cope with daily peaks the gas has to be more rapidly available than it is from aquifers or underground storage. Here 'line packing' is useful. This involves using the distribution network as an extension of the storage system:

If more gas is forced into the inlets of a high-pressure pipe than is being withdrawn at the outlets, the pressure increases and more gas is therefore stored. Conversely, if the offtake from the pipe exceeds the input, then pressure falls and gas is withdrawn from store.[2]

A further possibility is the use of liquefied natural gas (LNG) stored in refrigerated tanks or below-ground storage to meet sharp or unexpected peaks. In its liquid state natural gas reduces to one-six-hundredth of its gaseous volume so that a very substantial amount can be stored in a relatively small tank. The Gas Council is continuing to import LNG from Algeria and the Canvey Island storage tanks can hold five days' national consumption at 1967 rates, or about one to two days' national consumption by 1975.[3] Several other storage sites for LNG will be in operation by 1975, and these will either be supplied with Algerian LNG or with North Sea gas liquefied in special plants. Which method of storage will be used in a particular situation obviously

1. Aquifers are porous water-bearing rock strata into which the gas can be pumped under pressure, so driving out the water.
2. National Board for Prices and Incomes (1969), Report no. 102, *Gas Prices (Second Report)*, H.M.S.O., Cmnd 3974, p. 64.
3. *The Exploitation of North Sea Gas*, p. 38.

depends on the cost of storage and the balance between supply and demand, but the methods of supplying and storing natural gas seem better able to cope with peak demands than do those for manufactured town gas.

5. The Price of Natural Gas

Since the gas industry's major problem in the future will be to sell all the gas it has contracted to buy, a flexible price policy will be necessary. There will not be a single price for gas, but rather a range of prices depending on the amount taken, the conditions under which it is taken, and the effect of that particular demand on the industry's costs. However, in outlining some of the issues concerned with the pricing of North Sea gas, it is more convenient to begin the discussion in terms of an average price which ignores some of the complications of the price structure.

North Sea gas is purchased by the Gas Council at a landed price of 2·87d. per therm. Comparing this with the average net cost of manufactured gas – 10d. to 11d. per therm in 1968 – would seem to indicate that substantial price reductions will be possible for all consumers, but this is too simple a view. The Area Boards, which sell most gas, buy natural gas from the Gas Council at a bulk supply tariff which is uniform for all Boards. This tariff contains three elements:

a rental for each offtake point related to the cost of providing the connection; a maximum demand charge calculated by reference to each Board's peak day requirements fixed at such a level as will meet the transmission and other appropriate costs; a commodity charge based on price and load factor at the beach.[1]

Having bought gas, the Area Boards must then devise a structure of retail tariffs, and the principles on which these are based will differ between the premium and the non-premium markets.

When either the Gas Council or an Area Board is seeking to

1. *The Exploitation of North Sea Gas*, p.25.

sell gas to the non-premium market, the main issue is whether the price of gas is sufficiently low to compete with the other fuels, particularly coal and oil, since gas has few inherent advantages to the non-premium user. With a beachhead price of 2·87d. (1·20p) per therm the gas industry is obviously in a favourable position to compete for parts of the bulk market. Even when one takes into account distribution costs, the price per therm could still be competitive with coal and oil which sold to bulk users in 1968 at 4d. (1·67p)–6d. (2·5p) per therm. The I.C.I. contract mentioned earlier was based on a price of 4½d. (1·88p) per therm. So low a price was made possible by the size of the sale, the ease of distribution (I.C.I. could take the gas directly off the trunk distribution system), and the constant year-round demand which made for a significant improvement in the system load factor. These considerations – size of contract, cost of distribution, and effect on the industry's system load factor – will affect the price, as will the prices for other fuels. Press reports at the end of 1968 suggested that most of the initial industrial contracts were based on prices in the range 7d. (2·92p)–1s. (5p) per therm,[1] with 5d. (2·08p)–6d. (2·5p) as a possibility for interruptible sales.

Future gas prices in the premium domestic market are much more difficult to predict. Some Area Boards have already made small price reductions to consumers who have had appliances converted, but this seems largely to be in recompense for the inconvenience caused, and it is not clear what the longer-term trend of prices will be. One problem is the cost of conversion and of the new distribution and storage network. In the four years up to 1972/3 total investment will be £1221 million, and this will considerably increase depreciation and interest charges per therm. The cost of gas will fall as natural gas replaces manufactured gas, but over the period up to 1972/3 this may be counterbalanced by increases in other items of expenditure. Consequently, if the

1. In some cases, the gas industry would have to reduce its price to about 5d. (2·08p) or 6d. (2·5p) per therm to be competitive with coal and oil, but as the I.C.I. contract shows, it is prepared to do this when the contract terms are advantageous.

financial obligation of the industry remains 7 per cent net return on net assets as was the case in 1971/2, there may be little scope for price decreases. On the other hand, the gas industry's exploitation policy is based on low prices to stimulate demand, and the theoretical argument for lower prices is incontrovertible. Many economists, and the Select Committee on Nationalized Industries, take the view that the price of gas should be equated with the long-run marginal cost, i.e. with the extra cost of securing additional supplies of gas in the long run. The Prices and Incomes Board Report Appendix D discusses in detail the cost structure of the gas industry. Here we need only note that the long-run marginal cost of gas does not include the once-and-for-all cost of conversion, nor any depreciation charges on obsolescent town gas plants. Hence the long-run marginal cost of gas will be lower than present or future average costs which do include these components.

If the gas industry were to equate prices with long-run marginal costs, this would mean a rapid reduction in prices, but it would also mean that price per therm would be less than average cost per therm so that the industry did not cover its full accounting costs. On the other hand, to fix prices so that full accounting costs were covered and financial obligations met, might leave the industry little scope for price reductions at a time when it was trying to sell as much gas as possible. The Select Committee and the Prices and Incomes Board both suggested that this dilemma could be avoided by treating natural gas as an entirely new industry largely independent of the existing town gas industry. Then after 1970, when natural gas is a significant part of gas output, separate tariff policies could be developed and separate financial targets set for the natural gas industry, and in particular, natural gas prices could be set independently of any liabilities to the 'old' gas industry.

If the natural gas and the town gas industries were regarded as separate, this would also solve the problem of how to deal with the depreciation charges on obsolescent gas-making plant. There has been very heavy investment in this process since 1962/3, and in the period 1968–70 some £90 million was allocated to be spent on gas manufacturing plant to cope with increasing demand in areas where natural gas would not be available for some years. A penalty of the rapid switch to North Sea gas is that this plant will become prematurely obsolescent, before it has been written off under the industry's normal depreciation procedures. The depreciation charges still outstanding when the plants shut down are estimated to be £300 million. This £300 million is not a cost of supplying natural gas, and indeed in the economic sense it is not a 'cost' at all, since it is in respect of investment already made and involves no use of resources. However, it is an accounting charge, and must be provided for. If the 'two industries' argument were accepted, the capital liabilities of the town gas industry would fall on the remaining consumers of town gas or, more probably, on the taxpayer through a capital reconstruction involving the write-off of the obsolescent plant.

The Ministry of Power witnesses to the Select Committee considered that a capital reconstruction in respect of the obsolescent gas-making plants was not justifiable since the prospective earning power of the gas industry's total assets was very good. In April 1969 the Minister of Power decided that the industry should be responsible for paying off the £300 million depreciation charge, and that they should recover the cost from gas prices.[1] Though this would mean slightly higher gas prices, he considered that there would be no significant distortion of resource allocation. Indeed, the Gas Council calculated that the increase in costs as a result of paying off the £300 million would be less than $\frac{1}{2}$d. (0·21p) per therm in the peak year (about 3 per cent of the domestic tariff), declining as the plants were written off. In this particular instance, the effect of the higher price on the exploitation of natural gas would appear to be limited, but the general problem of pricing remains. The policy of rapid exploitation

1. Select Committee on Nationalized Industries (1969), *The Exploitation of North Sea Gas: Observations by the Minister of Power*, H.M.S.O., Cmnd 3996, p. 6.

depends on a very rapid growth of premium market demand and a considerable sale to the non-premium market, and these in turn depend on a competitive price for gas relative to other fuels. The industry therefore has to follow the logic of the exploitation policy in its pricing decisions, even if this has repercussions in the short-term on the financial obligation of the industry. As the Prices and Incomes Board commented:

what is important, however, from the point of view of reconciling the ... objectives of both covering accounting costs and reflecting in prices marginal costs is that the total financial target for the next few years should not be pitched at such a level as to inflict a long-term disadvantage in the marketing of natural gas.[1]

The Government is clearly aware of this problem, and though the setting of a separate financial target for natural gas has apparently been rejected, the financial objective over the period up to 1973/4.

will be consistent both with the earning of appropriate returns over the whole life of new assets ... and with the present and prospective situation facing the gas industry, including market conditions and the need for a rapid build-up in the use of North Sea gas.[2]

So far our discussion has concentrated on the general problem of pricing, and has been couched largely in terms of the average price paid. Another aspect of the pricing problem is the structure of prices. How much should particular consumers or groups of consumers pay for gas? Two factors are particularly important here. Firstly, consumers should as far as possible pay prices which reflect the cost of gas supplied to them; and secondly, the gas industry must take account of competitive fuel prices. The first point simply means that consumers who take gas in quantities and at times which lower the industry's costs should pay lower prices, whereas those whose consumption is sporadic and adds to the daily or seasonal peak ought to pay higher prices since they impose higher costs on the industry than regular or off-peak users. Of course, natural gas does not have to be produced in ex-

1. Prices and Incomes Board, Report no. 102, p. 18.
2. *Observations by the Minister of Power*, p. 6.

pensive plant as does electricity, and gas has the advantage
that it can be stored. Thus the difference in cost between peak
and off-peak gas may not be very great, but this depends on
how much it costs to store gas with which to meet peak
demand. The Prices and Incomes Board Report noted that a
rational and efficient tariff system should attempt to reflect
cost differences, and recommended experimentation with
alternative structures.

The second point, the level of competitive fuel prices, comes
into play in modifying the principle of charging according to
costs. The Ministry of Power has made it clear that the industry must cover its full accounting costs, and as we have seen,
this precludes charging prices equal to marginal cost. Instead,
prices must be 'related' to marginal costs, and the Minister
of Power in his observations on the Select Committee Report
concluded that the industry should have regard to what the
market would bear:

there are good grounds for charging prices close to long-run
marginal costs to those consumer classes that tend to be relatively
ensitive to price, while setting other parts of the industry's tariffs
ove marginal costs in order to make a contribution to the indus-
overheads. This is broadly the pricing policy which the gas
ry intends to pursue.[1]

ay, the industry hopes to fulfil its financial obliga-
at the same time achieve the rapid exploitation of
as.[2]

as industry was looking ahead to a future of
owth of sales, but as the foregoing discussion
ifficult to do more than report the forecasts
-1970s. The industry has stated what it

nister of Power, p.6.
1974, the industry's financial objective is
, equal to about 11·7 per cent gross. This
en greater efficiency from the industry if

would like to do, and the Government has devised a fuel policy within which the industry can grow. But circumstances can change, and the 1975 forecasts may not be borne out in practice. For example, these forecasts assumed that the electricity industry will burn 3400 million therms of natural gas, equivalent to 14 million tons of coal, but this will not happen, since the gas and electricity industries have been unable to agree on price and supply conditions. However, even in the absence of precise details, some conclusions on the future structure of the industry can be confidently predicted.

By 1975 the gas industry will in effect be a wholesaling organization, buying North Sea gas from the exploring companies and selling it to domestic, industrial and commercial users. The industry will be using no coal at all, all carbonization and Lurgi plants having been scrapped, and only about one-third as much oil as in 1968/9. Also, by 1975 the industry will be organized along rather different lines. The Area Boards were originally set up as independent units because they made and distributed their own gas. Since their manufacturing function will have virtually disappeared by 1975, and the industry's organization will be much more centralized und the British Gas Corporation, set up in 1972 to take over Gas Council's role.

The future success of the gas industry will depend ul on its marketing and commercial strategy and its increase sales so as to absorb the abundant sourc energy which natural gas provides. But, some ma happens when the existing reserves of gas are use possibilities exist. Firstly, more gas has been British sector, and further discoveries may be m substitute natural gas produced from oil r economic reality. The Gas Council has al process for making gas of a sufficiently but it is not economic compared with N natural gas could be imported. Enorm gas exist in Libya, Nigeria and elsew imported in liquid form as is Alge development of transportation me

constru...   ...NG could probably
be impo...   ...nother possible source
of impor...   ...sh sectors of the North
Sea. Cou...   ...not to exploit under-
sea discov...   ...rt their gas to Britain.
Most of t...   ...ditional gas would involve a
considerabl...   ...ayments cost, since they mean
importing eith...   ...as directly. However, it may be that
natural gas will simply be a transitional fuel. By the 1990s,
when the depletion period of North Sea reserves will be
nearing its end, there may be a new much cheaper source of
energy. In particular the generation of electricity in nuclear
power stations promises to be such a source, and the fast
...der reactor a... e possibility of power generation from
...n could leav... ural gas as a relatively high cost fuel by
... this eve... th Sea gas could be regarded simply as
... en the decline of one indigenous source
...he full development of another, nuclear

4 The Coal Industry

The post-war history of the coal industry falls into two distinct periods. Nationalized at the end of 1947, the industry went through a ten year period when its prime concern was to increase output at almost any cost. On the other hand, the decade 1957–67 was one of virtually continuous decline in demand and output, with the industry struggling to withstand the growing competition from other fuels.

This chapter is in four sections. Section 1 gives a broad picture of the industry's progress over the post-war period and the main reasons for the decline after 1957, section looks at the improved productivity of the industry over decade up to 1967/8 and how this was attained, sect covers the cost structure of the industry, its pricing and its financial performance, and section 4 looks a policy for the industry.

1. Demand and Output since Nationalization

The period between nationalization and 195 acute coal shortage, with the productive industry fully stretched. Pits were generall geological reasons, new pits were opened, i equipment and reconstruction was hig Coal Board's main problem was tha enormous efforts of the industry we demand. Some coal was importe States, while coal was not full 1950s. Undistributed stocks a were low up to about 1957 than two million tons, equivalent to less than one week's consumption. Undistributed plus distributed stocks were, on average, equivalent to around five weeks of consumption. British fuel policy became geared to coal-saving measures. The railways were encouraged to switch to diesel traction, the nuclear energy programme was instituted, and industry was urged to economize on its use of coal. This first decade after nationalization was therefore characterized by continuous attempts to expand output, and in 1956/7 the industry was aiming for a target output of 240 million tons per annum by 1965. However, 1957/8 saw a change in the industry's fortunes. Starting with the industrial recession of 1958 followed by intense competition from other fuels as well as rapid improvements in coal-burning methods, the industry began to decline. After a rapid increase in stockbuilding,[1] output and employment began to decline, as did the industry's share of the energy market. Table 13 shows these changes with data for the years 1947, 1957 and 1967. In spite of its decline, the industry in 1967 still satisfied the greater proportion of the nation's energy requirements, and by any standards the National Coal Board is a huge undertaking. In 1967/8 it was the biggest employer in Western Europe, its wage bill amounted to about £8 million per week, its turnover was in excess of £800 million per annum, while its capital expenditure between 1960 and 1967 ran at about £80 million per annum.

The demand for coal and the structure of this demand have undergone considerable changes over the post-war period. Table 14 shows the principal markets for coal in the three years 1947, 1957 and 1967. The general picture is quite clear. Between 1947 and 1957, the rapid growth of demand from the electricity industry and coke ovens was more than enough to offset the slight decline in coal used by the railways and miscellaneous markets. Other markets, including the

1. Undistributed stocks rose from 8·6 million tons in 1957 to 19·7 million tons in 1958 and 35·7 million tons in 1959. At the end of 1967 they stood at 27·7 million tons. Adding to stocks cost the N.C.B. about 15s (75 p) per ton to lay down in the first year and 5s (25p) per ton per annum thereafter.

Table 13
Coal Output, Employment and Energy Share 1947, 1957, 1967
(calendar years)

	1947	1957	1967
Coal output (million tons)[1]	197·4	223·7	172·2
Wage earners employed in N.C.B. mines ('000)[2]	701·5	703·8	401·1
Coal's share of inland energy consumption (coal consumption as percentage of total inland fuel consumption in coal equivalent)[3]	70·7	86·5	55·4

Notes: 1. This includes output from opencast mines which in the three years 1947, 1957 and 1967 was 10·2, 13·6 and 7·1 million tons respectively. It also includes the small amounts of output from licensed mines and tips.

2. This covers only wage earners on colliery books. It excludes other employees – administrative, technical and clerical – employed at mines and headquarters. These amounted to nearly 60,000 in 1967.

3. Total inland energy consumption excludes the consumption of electricity other than that generated in hydroelectric and nuclear stations. It also excludes the consumption of gas other than natural gas and methane.

Source: Ministry of Power, *Statistical Digest 1967*.

important industrial and domestic sectors, were more or less constant. However, between 1957 and 1967 a decline was experienced in all markets bar electricity. Those markets which had been declining before 1957 declined even more swiftly after 1957, and the growth in demand from the electricity industry, which was slower than before, was insufficient to counterbalance the other lost markets. The most obvious consequence of this was that total coal consumption fell by about 25 per cent between 1957 and 1967 and the pattern of demand for coal altered quite markedly. In particular the electricity industry became a very much more important customer, accounting for 41 per cent of total consumption in 1967 as against 21 per cent in 1957.

Table 14

Consumption of Coal 1947, 1957 and 1967: Million Tons

	1947	1957	1967
Electricity supply industry	27·1	46·4	66·6
Gas supply industry	22·7	26·4	14·4
Coke ovens	19·8	30·7	23·1
Domestic	35·8	35·6	23·0
Industry	36·0	37·5	20·1
Railways	14·3	11·4	0·8
Collieries	11·0	7·2	2·9
Miscellaneous	15·3	14·9	10·9
Overseas and Northern Ireland	7·8	10·7	4·0
Total consumption and shipments	189·8	220·8	165·8

Note: The difference between the output figures in Table 13 and the figures above is explained by imports and stock changes.

Source: Ministry of Power, *Statistical Digest 1967*.

The decline of coal markets between 1957 and 1967 occurred at a time when total inland energy consumption was rising, though not as rapidly as in the early 1950s. It is all the more interesting, therefore, to ask why coal was losing its markets. There are three factors which caused the decline in coal markets and, in the case of electricity, a rise in consumption which was not as fast as it had previously been. Firstly, though perhaps least important, many of the major industrial coal users were themselves declining or stagnating; secondly, there was a more efficient use of coal; and thirdly, and most important, there was an increase in the substitution of other fuels for coal. These influences were of course also present before 1957, but generally to a lesser degree. All three factors are to some extent interdependent, and it is impossible to say exactly how much of the over-all decline was caused by each.

The fact that many of the large coal-using industries declined or grew only very slowly in the period up to 1968 obviously reduced the demand for coal below what it otherwise would have been. For example, railways, textiles and metal manufacture were important users of coal in the 1950s but their consumption fell rapidly in the decade up to 1968. The very large fall in consumption by these industries cannot however be explained entirely by their decline or stagnation of output. In these industries, as in all others, there was a trend towards a more efficient use of coal and a massive switch to alternative fuels.

It is obvious that any fuel user will try to extract as much energy from the fuel as is economically possible. On the whole coal, and indeed other fuels, have been used much more efficiently over the past decade. This is particularly true of coal used in steam raising where technological, metallurgical and design improvements have increased the thermal efficiency of the equipment.[1] The average thermal efficiency of conventional steam power stations increased from 21·1 per cent in 1948 to 25·9 per cent in 1958, and 27·9 per cent in 1967. The latter figure would have been higher had it not been for technical difficulties encountered by the electricity industry with some of their very big generating sets. Even so, the seemingly quite small change from 1958 to 1967 meant that the electricity industry used about five million tons of coal less in 1967 than would have been the case if the thermal efficiency of stations had remained at the 1958 level. The thermal efficiency of industrial boilers also rose and this tended to reduce the industrial market for coal. About 75 per cent of industrial coal is used for steam-raising purposes. The iron and steel industry was another market where demand fell, in part as a result of greater efficiency in the use of fuel. The industry in the mid-1960s was using almost 25 per cent less coke to produce a ton of pig iron than it was in the mid-1950s.

The most important factor in explaining the fall in demand for coal has been the substitution of other fuels for coal. Both domestic and industrial consumers have been switching from solid fuel to electricity, gas and oil. In the industrial markets, price competition has been the major reason for

1. Thermal efficiency is the calorific value or heat output of the fuel as a proportion of the calorific value of the fuel used.

this switching, though the competitor fuels, mainly oil and gas, have other advantages in ease of handling and storage, cleanliness and controllability. The decline in the domestic markets has probably been more a result of these non-price factors together with the attractive image projected by the gas and electricity industries in their advertising campaigns. The Clean Air Act of 1956 and the massive slum clearance operations of the 1950s and 1960s are also very important in explaining the declining domestic demand. Most of the old houses which were cleared used coal for heating and perhaps also for cooking, while the new houses either did not use coal at all or used it much more efficiently.

At the same time that this switch away from coal was taking place at the level of final demand, the market situation was seriously aggravated by an increasing usage of other primary fuels by the secondary fuel industries, gas and electricity. The gas industry was rapidly switching to oil-gasification in the 1960s and in 1968 was beginning to take supplies of natural gas. In 1967 the gas industry was using about 9·4 million tons coal equivalent more oil than in 1957. The electricity industry was generating increasing amounts in nuclear and oil-fired stations between 1957 and 1967, and in 1967 it used 67 million tons of coal and coke and 11·0 million tons coal equivalent of oil, as compared with 46·5 and 1·0 million tons respectively in 1957. Also, in 1967 21·3 GWh of electricity were generated in nuclear stations, equivalent to about 9 million tons of coal, as against virtually nothing in 1957. A rough estimate is that without the increased use of other fuels, the electricity industry would have used about 20 million more tons of coal in 1967 than was actually the case.

The decline in the demand for coal would undoubtedly have been much greater if the Government had not evolved various measures to protect the industry. Coal imports were banned between 1959 and 1970 and in 1961 a duty was put on fuel oil at the rate of 2d. (0·83p) per gallon – about £2 per ton and equivalent to at least 25s. (£1·25p) per ton protection of coal. In 1968 the fuel oil duty was 2·42d. (1·01p) per gallon. There were also pressures on the electricity and gas industries to slow down their switch to alternative fuels, and the industries have largely accepted such pressures, though in the case of the gas industry the effect has been very small. Under the Coal Industry Act 1967, the electricity industry was to burn up to 6 million tons of coal per annum over and above what it would have burnt on purely commercial considerations. The industry was compensated for the extra costs incurred and the arrangement remained in operation until 1971. A final aspect of protection for the coal industry is that Government buildings and establishments are obliged to use coal for heating purposes except where the benefits of using alternative fuels are more than marginal, usually where the cost differentials are in excess of 5 per cent. It was hoped that local authorities would follow this example.

It would be wrong to suggest that the coal industry faced the decline of its markets with equanimity or was prepared to rest under the umbrella of protection. In the ten years up to 1968, the industry made strenuous efforts to adjust itself to the new market situations and to improve its competitive position. The growth in productivity was very impressive, as the next section shows.

2. Productivity in the Coal Industry

Productivity in the industry is usually measured by output per manshift. This grew slowly between 1947 and 1957, from 22 cwt to 25 cwt, but by 1967/8 it had increased to 39 cwt. This latter increase in productivity took place in spite of shorter hours per shift and in spite of increased absenteeism.[1] Two major related factors explain the coal industry's good productivity record between 1957 and 1968; firstly, the concentration of output on pits and faces capable of higher levels of productivity, and secondly, the increased mechanization in the industry.

Even before 1957, output was being concentrated in the

1. Absenteeism among underground workers increased from 15 per cent in 1957 to 17·8 per cent in 1967. The rate of absenteeism in 1968 was one of the highest in British industry.

better pits and poor pits were being closed. The National Coal Board took over 958 collieries in 1947 and this number had been reduced to 822 in 1957. The greater part of these closures were, however, not principally for economic reasons, but because the pits were exhausted. After 1957 the rundown speeded up and pits were closed not simply because they were exhausted but because they were uneconomic and not capable of sufficiently high levels of productivity. Between 1964 and 1968 the industry closed down collieries at the rate of around one a week, and by the end of 1968 was working only 330 collieries. The rundown was particularly severe in Scotland and Lancashire with output being concentrated on the high-productivity collieries in Yorkshire and the East Midlands.

Not only has there been a concentration on fewer pits but also on fewer coal faces. The number of major faces being worked in late 1968 was about 1000, less than half of the number in 1963 and only slightly more than the number of collieries being worked in 1947. Concentration on fewer faces gives greater ease of organization and greater prospects of using machinery and equipment more fully, but not all faces were equally productive. About fifty faces were producing more than 450 tons a shift compared with the national average of 255 tons but about one-third of the faces were producing under 200 tons. This shows that in spite of the concentration on fewer faces and the abandoning of poor faces, the industry still had a considerable number of low-productivity faces.

The rundown of collieries was carried out by the industry with considerable concern for its labour force and with every attempt to avoid redundancy. Miners in pits that were to be closed were generally offered employment in nearby pits or in the Yorkshire or Midlands pits. Generous allowances were available for miners prepared to move outside their old district,[1] though initially most new work offered was within daily travelling distance. However, by 1967/8 the easy transfers had already taken place, and the acceleration of closures

1. Allowances include removal and travel expenses, settlement grants and a rent allowance for seven years if rents are higher than in their old district.

was accompanied by higher redundancy.[1] In anticipation of this trend, the Coal Industry Act 1967 provided that redundant miners aged over fifty-five could have their incomes supplemented for three years giving them an income during this period of about 90 per cent of their previous take-home pay. They receive their normal pensions after this period even if still under the normal retirement age of sixty-five.

The rundown of the industry increased its productivity and level of performance but it has also given rise to problems, particularly on the labour side. One has been the disadvantageous effects of the rapid rundown on morale. This has had expression in the considerable problems of recruitment and wastage. Young men are not particularly willing to enter the industry in view of the uncertain future it appears to face, and recruitment of juveniles fell from 13,000 in 1961 to 7500 in 1967. Recruitment problems, reluctance of many men to stay in the industry when collieries were closed plus a movement out of the industry by men under forty, have all meant that the average age in the industry has been continually rising. The average age of wage earners in 1967 was 43·7 as against 41·6 in 1960. About 64 per cent of wage earners were over the age of forty and about 38 per cent were over fifty. The difficulties of recruiting younger men for craft training and of keeping young skilled workers are particularly serious insofar as mechanization has increased, and will continue to increase, the need for these groups.[2]

The second major explanation of the rapid increase of productivity in the industry has been the increase in mechani-

1. The generous provisions of the Redundancy Payments Act made miners less inclined to accept transfers to distant collieries.
2. During the late 1960s the rundown of the coal industry caused relatively few industrial relations problems. The trade unions view the rundown as being largely beyond the control of the Coal Board, and labour–management co-operation has been close at all levels. An example of this is that the number of strikes in the coal industry fell dramatically during the period 1957–68 when the national trend of work stoppages was upwards. The number of stoppages in the industry fell from 2224 in 1957 to 219 in 1968, representing 78 per cent and 9 per cent respectively of total work stoppages recorded by the Department of Employment and Productivity.

zation. It would be wrong to think that the industry was not mechanized in 1947. Even at that date about 75 per cent of the industry's output was cut and conveyed mechanically. The figure had risen to about 90 per cent by 1957. The major change in mechanization, however, has been in the use of power loaders.[1] The percentage of output which was power loaded increased from 2·4 per cent in 1947 to 15 per cent in 1956 and 91 per cent in March 1968. Concomitant with the increased use of power loaders has been the extension of hydraulically powered roof supports. About 62 per cent of major longwall faces had these by March 1968. The next stage in mechanization was expected to be the Remotely Operated Longwall Face (ROLF) system. This system involves power loading and advancing roof supports controlled by a console away from the face itself. The Board had used the system on experimental faces in 1963 and 1964 In 1965 it was decided to try the system under normal conditions in the Bevercotes colliery. The system gave good results for a year until serious geological faults halted operations. Production did not recommence until mid 1971. There are still unresolved technical problems with ROLF. A more major problem is that, at Bevercotes at least, the men have declined to work a seven day week, necessary if the system is to be economic.

Technical developments in the industry have not been limited to the face itself. Communications between face and surface have been improved as has winding machinery at the shaft. Trucks and conveyor belts have been increasingly used to

1. It may be appropriate to describe briefly the coalmining methods currently in use. The vast majority of coal is mined on the advancing longwall face system using power loaders and powered supports. In this system a shearing drum cuts along a face usually about 600 ft. long. On each traverse (or 'strip'), the shearer cuts about two feet into the face, and the coal thereby dislodged is thrown on to a conveyor belt running along the face and thence on to another belt which runs along the exit roadway to the shaft. As the shearer traverses, powered hydraulic supports holding the roof are advanced singly or in batches. The roof is allowed to collapse behind the supports. A fuller account of mining techniques can be found in *Fuel Policy*, Appendix IV.

speed up the transport of men and materials to and from the face. On the surface there have been extensive developments in wagon loading and coal preparation.

The coal industry's aim was to make even greater productivity gains up to 1970/71, when the planned level of output from all mechanized faces was expected to be 500 tons per shift compared with the March 1968 level of 234 tons. This target output amounted to 50 cwt per manshift, and the eventual aim was 75 cwt per manshift in 1975. Certainly there is scope for large productivity gains in the industry. Improved machine utilization in particular could make a substantial contribution. In 1966, power loaders were only being used for 125 minutes out of the 350 minutes possible running time per shift.[1] Some of the lost running time was a result of unforeseeable factors but much was caused by poor organization. Every minute of additional running time would have given the coal industry a million tons of extra coal at little extra cost. The industry is very conscious of the problem of machine utilization and in general the lack of adequate exploitation of its present advanced equipment. Since 1967 it has organized training courses specifically aimed at getting big increases in face productivity through better organization and machine utilization, and by 1969 there had been considerable improvements. Very detailed planning of faces is now becoming common in the industry, and there is a recognition, perhaps belated, that each face is equivalent to a small or medium sized business. A face producing 500 tons a shift has an annual turnover of about £1¼ million.

A comparison of the British productivity with that in the United States appears to confirm that the British coal industry has a large potential for increased productivity, since the United States coal industry produces 800–1000 tons per shift. Certain technical and geological reasons partly explain this. The U.S. coal industry enjoys thicker, less faulted, more even and more horizontal seams than does the British industry. At the same time the seams are at a shallower depth. This makes for greater ease of communications and reduces costs of

1. Platt, J. (1968), *British Coal*, Lyon, Grant & Green, p. 97.

ventilation and pumping. It also allows different techniques of longwall face mining which increase productivity. However part of the difference in output per shift is explained by poorer organization and perhaps a lower level of productivity consciousness in the British collieries.[1]

3. Costs, Prices and Financial Performance

The considerable growth of productivity in the industry has not enabled it to stabilize costs and prices, and both have risen rapidly over the post-war period. Table 15 shows the average cost per saleable ton of coal and its main components in 1948, 1958 and 1967/8.

Table 15
Cost per Ton of Saleable Output

	1948		1958		1967/8	
	s. d.	%	s. d.	%	s. d.	%
Wages and related costs	30 6 (£1·52)	67	49 8 (£2·48)	59	49 3 (£2·46)	51
Materials, repairs, power	9 11 (£0.50)	22	19 9 (£0·99)	24	23 2 (£1·15)	24
Depreciation	1 6 (£0·08)	3	4 0 (£0·20)	5	5 3 (£0·26)	6
Other costs	3 7 (£0·18)	8	10 6 (£0·52)	12	18 3 (£0·91)	19
Total	45 6 (£2·28)	100	83 11 (£4·19)	100	95 11 (£4·79)	100

Note: The 1966/7 total cost was 98/5d. per ton. The reduction in 1967/8 was due to large decreases in wages and depreciation. The reduced depreciation provision, totalling £11·9 million, came about because of the capital reconstruction of the industry.
Source: National Coal Board, *Annual Reports*.

1. Following the national power loading agreement of 1966, the great majority of British miners are paid on day wage, not piecework. While this agreement represented a major breakthrough in industrial relations, the recent slowdown in productivity growth suggests that some incentive scheme based on productivity might now be advisable (see p. 105).

The table demonstrates clearly that the mechanization and closure programme was able to stabilize labour costs per ton in the second decade compared with the experience of the first ten years. The proportion of total costs made up by wage costs fell considerably between 1958 and 1967/8 though the industry was still very labour-intensive. The apparent slow rise in depreciation expenditure in spite of the extensive modernization programme is to a large extent explained by the capital reconstruction of the industry under the Coal Industry Act 1965. This relieved the industry of £415 million of its capital debt, of which £404 million had been charged by March 1968. Consequently the depreciation provision fell, and some idea of the importance of this can be gained from the fact that the depreciation charge in 1963/4, before the reconstruction began, was 6s. 10d. (34·17p) per ton, almost 8 per cent of the average cost per ton. Other important factors which have at least contained the rise in depreciation costs over the last decade have been the savings on equipment arising out of the concentration of output on fewer pits and faces plus a considerable growth in the hiring, as opposed to the purchase, of plant.[1] The hiring of plant and equipment is included in the 'other costs' shown in Table 15 and in part explains the rapid growth of these costs between 1958 and 1967/8. Administrative costs, pension provisions and local rates, included in the category 'other costs', also rose rapidly.

The average operating cost figure of about 96s. (£4·80) a ton in 1967/8 disguised the fact that there were considerable variations in the actual cost of mining coal, with large amounts of coal being produced at costs well below and well above the average. In considering cost differences we must take account of the calorific value or heat output of the coal, since the coal industry is actually selling heat. It is therefore best to express the cost of coal in terms of pence per therm. At the 1967/8 average cost per ton of just under 100s. (£5) (pit-

1. Expenditure on hired plant was about £1·4 million in 1957 and £8·5 million in 1967/8. The hiring of transport facilities also reduced depreciation expenditure. Transport hiring expenditure rose from about £2 million in 1957 to £7 million in 1967/8.

head prices), the average cost per therm was about 5d. (2·08p). It is estimated however, that in 1966/7 over sixty million tons was produced at below 4d. (1·67p) per therm, of which about ten million tons was below 3d. (1·25p) per therm. But nearly ten million tons was being mined at more than 6d. (2·5p) per therm. As a result of increased mechanization and the closure of high-cost pits and faces, the differences in costs over the range of the industry's output had probably lessened by 1969. At the end of the 1960s the industry estimated that it would be producing coal at an average cost of 1·67p a therm by the mid-1970s and that around seventy million tons would be produced at 1·35p per therm. The intention was to use this seventy million tons in power station and general industrial markets in order to secure big, long-term contracts, and certainly coal at a pithead price of 3¼d. (1·35p) per therm would be highly competitive with all fuels except untaxed fuel oil.

The variations in cost per therm, or cost per ton of mining coal, can be explained by differences in the costs of mining particular types of coal and by area cost differences, though the two are not unrelated. Coking coals, large coals and anthracite cost above the average to mine, because the geological conditions tend to be difficult and this limits the prospect of high levels of mechanization. Steam-raising coals on the other hand can often be mined in highly mechanized pits and cost below average to produce. Area differences in costs, though falling as the industry is rationalized and mechanization becomes more widespread, are still considerable. In 1967/8, cost per ton ranged from 77s. 4d. (£3·87) in South Midlands and 78s. (£3·90) in North Notts. to 125s. 3d. (£6·26) in Kent and 133s. 8d. (£6·68) in West Wales.[1] These

1. The areas mentioned are part of a new administrative structure which the N.C.B. adopted in 1967. The earlier five-tier system of N.C.B., Divisions, Areas, Groups and collieries was replaced by a three-tier system which increased the size of the Areas and omitted the Divisions and Groups. The restructuring was an attempt to prevent the smaller industry (relative to the 1950s) 'being saddled with more harness than horse'. The new Areas enjoy considerable autonomy and are big by normal business standards. An average Area employs about 20,000 men and has a turnover of about £50 million per annum.

differences are a result of many factors, but the most important, however, is again undoubtedly geological conditions – depth, slope, thickness and straightness of seam plus the incidence of faulting. But other explanatory factors are differences in absenteeism, extent of multi-shift working, degree of mechanization (often decided by geological conditions) and levels of organization at the pits and faces.

In spite of these considerable variations in costs, the pricing policy adopted by the National Coal Board does not fully reflect the differences in costs between various coals and areas.[1] Until recently the pithead price of industrial coal was its calorific value multiplied by a national price per calorific unit and then adjusted. This price is adjusted according to size and preparation, sulphur and ash content and a coalfield adjustment. Since 1954, the industry has also made 'selective adjustments' both for particular types of coal which cost more to mine and in respect of high-cost areas, but during the 1950s, the Board tended to follow a policy of average cost pricing under which price increases were of a general percentage kind. During the 1960s, selective adjustments became more common, but a Prices and Incomes Board report in 1966 suggested that the industry had not gone far enough with its selective adjustments, and recommended that prices should be more closely related to costs in individual production areas.[2]

The N.C.B. has revised its price policy since 1966 and great emphasis has been laid on the need for flexibility, expecially in the electricity and industrial markets, where the coal industry is anxious to negotiate long-term contracts. In addition, in 1970, it introduced a pricing system based on area, rather than national, costs per unit. This was aimed at

1. The determination of coal prices is complicated. The description in the text is only to give a general picture of the factors involved. For more details see Confederation of British Industry, *Coal: The Price Structure 1966.* For post-1970 pricing see National Board for Prices and Incomes (1971), Report no. 153, *Coal Prices Second Report (Supplement no. 1)*, H.M.S.O., Cmnd 4455–1.

2. National Board for Prices and Incomes (1966), Report no. 12, *Coal Prices*, H.M.S.O., Cmnd 2919.

reducing the inter-area cross-subsidisation and distortions of thermal relativities in the earlier system. However, on a more general basis the N.C.B. has rejected any suggestion that it move towards marginal cost pricing or individual colliery pricing, on the grounds that this would be 'incompatible with relative price stability or rational distribution',[1] given the variation in costs over time and between collieries supplying the same markets. The Board's principle is therefore to fix 'relative prices as between coalfields in a manner which reflects the average efficiency of working in each coalfield', and hence to move towards a pricing structure which is more closely related to costs. It would seem, though, that what is in essence a differentiated average cost pricing structure will still result in some cross-subsidization, certainly within coalfields, and also between coalfields insofar as prices do not fully reflect cost differences. In theory this would mean that output from high-cost pits would be sold at too low a price, with an artificial stimulation of demand for that output, whereas coal from the low-cost modern pits would be sold at too high a price. In consequence, there would be some misallocation of resources. In practice, this judgement must be qualified. A study of the industry over the period 1948–61 suggested that

the National Coal Board's long-run allocation decisions (on output and investment) have not been generally distorted by the presence of some cross-subsidising at each point in time. Broadly speaking, the Coal Board has been able to determine which pits and areas need expanding or closing in conformance with probable long-run efficiency.[2]

It seems probable that the accelerated rundown in the 1960s has taken similar account of efficient allocation of resources.

In the past, the fact that prices did not fully reflect costs has meant that some regions have seldom broken even. Thus the Kent, South-Western and North-Western Divisons have made a surplus, after charging depreciation and interest, in

1. *Ministerial Control of the Nationalised Industries*, vol. 3, p. 227.

2. Shepherd, W. G. (1964), 'Cross-subsidising and allocation in public firms', *Oxford Economic Papers*; abridged as 'Cross-subsidisation in coal' in *Public Enterprise*, p. 346.

only one year since vesting day, and the Scottish and Northumberland/Durham Divisions have done only slightly better with three surplus years each. The East Midlands Division by contrast has never been in deficit. Unlike other nationalized industries, the coal industry as a whole does not have a target rate of return on net assets. Instead it is enjoined 'to break even after interest and depreciation including £10 million to cover the difference between depreciation at historic cost and replacement cost'.[1] During 1965/6 and 1966/7 the National Coal Board was temporarily relieved of this objective but it was revived in 1967/8. In that year however, the industry made a surplus of only £400,000 and though this was its best performance for four years, was unable to meet the £10 million depreciation target. In 1969/70 and 1970/71, the Board was given the target of breaking even, after interest and depreciation. This was waived during the coal strike year of 1971/2.

4. Future Policy towards the Coal Industry

Government policy for coal over the period to 1975, as expressed in the Fuel Policy White Paper of 1967, makes very gloomy reading.[2] It anticipates continued decline of the industry in terms of output and employment, but makes the point that 'this is not the result of Governmental policy, it reflects a continuing trend in consumer preferences'.[3] The Government was not, however, prepared to see the industry decline too swiftly. Protective policies continued to be operated by both Labour and Conservative Governments and, indeed, under the latter were considerably intensified in December, 1972 (see pp. 104–105). Policy is obviously pulled between sympathy for an industry which is important both politically and economically, and the need to pursue an economic fuel policy. 'We cannot afford to penalize our

1. *Nationalized Industries: A Review of Economic and Financial Objectives*, p. 16.
2. Plans for the fuel sector including coal can be found in *Fuel Policy*.
3. ibid., p. 44.

competitive standing as a nation by adding unnecessarily to our energy costs. Developments in recent years have reduced our competitive advantage in fuels *vis-a-vis* Europe.'[1]

British fuel policy to 1975 has been largely based on the likely energy demands shown in Table 16 below.

Table 16
Trends of Primary Fuel Use

| | Million tons of coal or coal equivalent | | | |
	1957 (actual)	1966 (actual)	1970	1975
Coal	212·9	174·7	152	120
Oil	36·7	111·7	125	145
Nuclear and hydro-electricity	1·7	10·2	16	35
Natural gas	—	1·1	17	50
Total inland demand	251·3	297·7	310	350

Source: *Fuel Policy*, pp. 36, 49.

The very considerable fall in demand between 1966 and 1975 was expected to be largely a result of serious declines in the industry's domestic, industrial and gasworks markets. The latter was expected to be consuming no coal in 1975 as against 17 million tons in 1966, while domestic consumption of coal was expected to fall from 27·5 to 15 million tons and industrial consumption from 25·2 to 9 million tons. Demand by the electricity industry was expected to remain fairly constant, at 65 million tons in 1975 as against 69 million tons in 1966.

There was not much dispute about the 1970 estimates of coal consumption. The Coal Board was fully consulted, and largely accepted the conclusions of the Government's fuel policy. It was the 1975 estimates which caused most trouble, and here the Board in its Report for 1967/8 flatly registered 'disagreement with the longer-term policy' (para. 18). One

1. *Fuel Policy*, p. 41.

must be clear what the 1975 forecast of 120 million tons meant. It meant a rundown between 1970 and 1975 faster in percentage terms than that between 1968 and 1970 and the disappearance, according to the Coal Board, of 115,000 jobs between 1971 and 1975/6, with the industry employing only 160,000 at the latter date compared with 365,000 in 1968. By 1975 coal would be taking second place to oil as a primary fuel source, with about 30 per cent of the market as against 40 per cent for oil. At the same time, the *Fuel Policy* White Paper gave the industry notice that after 1971 it would be expected to compete without the special measures provided under the Coal Industry Acts. The period up to 1971 was quite clearly regarded as transitional. In the event this proved to be optimistic and assistance was continued after 1971.[1]

A prime question was whether the estimates made by the Government represented an accurate picture of how the coal industry could perform in 1975, or whether the Coal Board was correct in its more optimistic forecasts that the 1975 market for coal was about 135 million tons.[2] In general, criticism of the Ministry of Power's 1975 estimates centred around three main questions. Firstly, were the total energy estimates right; secondly, could the coal industry increase its performance to such an extent that its competitiveness would give it a bigger market than 120 million tons; and thirdly, was a fuel policy which ran the coal industry down to 120 million tons the right sort of energy policy for Britain.

The 1975 total energy demand estimate in the White Paper is based on a forecast growth rate of GDP of 3 per cent per annum. It also appears to be based on an assumed energy

1. The Labour Government's assistance for the coal industry was largely continued by the Conservative Government and indeed extended in 1972 (see pp. 104–105).
2. In evidence to the Select Committee on Nationalized Industries in March 1969 Lord Robens stated that the coal industry could sell more to the electricity industry in 1975 than the Government estimates allowed. His estimate was that the coal industry would have sales of 77 million tons to the electricity industry rather than 65 million tons as estimated in the *Fuel Policy* White Paper. He also expected coal exports to be higher than had previously been estimated.

coefficient of 0·8.[1] Any upward revision of these assumptions would have a considerable effect on the total energy demands and thus possibly also on the demand for coal. If, for example, the growth of GDP were 4 per cent instead of 3 per cent, total energy demand would be about 13·4 million tons above the 1975 estimate of 350 million tons. If the demand for coal remained the same proportion of total energy demand, the additional market for coal would be around 4·6 million tons. A growth of GDP at 3·2 per cent per annum (about the rate 1960/64) would give an additional demand for coal of under one million tons. The White Paper considered, however, that coal markets were unlikely to be sensitive to variations in the rate of growth of the economy:

although in conditions of fast expansion the total demand for fuel would be higher, coal's proportional share might be lower, if only because the industry would probably have to pay higher wages to retain the necessary manpower, with adverse effect on prices, (p. 61).

It is difficult to know how far this would be the case.

The White Paper makes no mention of the energy coefficient *per se*, but from the figures available it would appear that an estimate of around 0·8 was used. This is above the actual coefficient for the period 1951–62 (0·52), and above the forecast for the period to 1975 used by some other observers. A coefficient of 0·7 was used in the Beckerman survey of likely future developments in the British economy.[2] Beckerman's figure was expected to be a result of much greater levels of mechanization in industry with a consequential increase in energy consumption per unit of output, plus in the domestic markets 'a rather more marked trend than over the period 1951–62 towards better heated homes.' There is no explanation in the White Paper as to why the Ministry chose such a high energy coefficient. In the event,

1. The energy coefficient measures the relation between the growth of Gross Domestic Product and the growth of energy demand measured in coal equivalent. It is the percentage increase in energy consumption resulting from a one per cent increase in Gross Domestic Product.

2. Beckerman, W., *et al.* (1965), *The British Economy in 1975*, Cambridge University Press.

the energy coefficient in the years after the White Paper, though erratic, was higher than the Ministry forecast.

The future level of demand for coal not only depends on total energy requirements but also on how competitive coal becomes *vis-a-vis* alternative fuels. This is also extremely difficult to predict, depending as it does on the increase in productivity which the coal industry can achieve, the extent to which this is absorbed by increased costs, the changes in other fuel prices, and the type of economic policies followed by the Coal Board and the Government. Certainly if the industry attained its target of seventy to eighty million tons of industrial and electricity coal at 1·35p per therm and an average price for all coals of 1·67p per therm by 1975, and if costs could be progressively reduced up to 1975, the industry would be in a strongly competitive position in the industrial and electricity markets. In the domestic market, the industry hoped to capture a larger share principally through the introduction in 1969 of a central heating system which can burn bituminous coal smokelessly. Such a system has very low fuel costs relative to other central heating systems. It is, however, the industrial and electricity markets, and particularly the latter, which really matter to the industry in the future.

In the electricity market, various arguments concerning coal's competitiveness have been put forward by the various parties and the conclusions are not clear. Essentially, in the late 1960s, the industry believed that it could supply on a long-term contract to the electricity industry at 3¼d. (1·35p) per therm: the electricity industry did not accept this, nor did the Ministry of Power who used a higher figure (reportedly 4¼d. (1·88p)) in calculating the cost of a coal power station at Seaton Carew, which is in fact to be nuclear. On the basis of present policy and cost estimates, it must be doubtful whether any more coal-fired stations are justified on economic grounds. The electricity industry will still, of course, continue to burn coal in existing coal-fired stations but as the coal-fired stations become older, they will have a lower merit order rating and be used less frequently. Without new coal-fired capacity, the demand for coal by the electricity industry will fall after the mid-1970s. The coal industry's long-term future is therefore very much tied up with those decisions by the electricity industry on what type of capacity it installs. The Coal Board's view was not only that it can offer very low-priced coal which would make it competitive with the new advanced gas-cooled reactor (AGR) power stations, but also that the AGR stations were based on a very new technology and that the then current cost estimates might be much too low.[1]

The third important criticism made by the Coal Board and others was that the 1975 Government estimates of the market for coal did not appear to be based on a 'total sum' approach. This approach involves attempting to find the right energy mix taking all costs into account – social as well as commercial – for all affected sectors of the economy. In 1968 an independent study of the energy sector, commissioned by the N.C.B., was published by the Economist Intelligence Unit.[2] This looked at the costs and disadvantages of running the coal industry down to 120 million tons, and appraised the effects on the railways, on the export potential of the mining machinery industry, the social costs to the coal industry and the nation of redeployment and employment of redundant miners, the costs arising out of the speedy write-off of machinery, the effect on the balance of payments of using other fuels, and so on. The report attempted, on the basis of such an approach, to find the best fuel mix, and concluded that the most efficient policy would leave coal with an inland market of 144 million tons in 1975. The Ministry of Power, however, rejected this study as being erroneous in several respects, and emphasised that the fuel policy was in fact based on a 'total sum' approach.[3]

1. Here, the Coal Board was proved right. Four of the five AGR stations building in 1972 had encountered serious technological and constructional problems which are delaying completion. Heysham, started in 1970, has only been delayed slightly. But Dungeness B, started in 1966 now has an expected completion date of 1975 – only one year before Heysham. Inevitably these delays and problems have increased the cost of the AGR programme.
2. Economist Intelligence Unit (May 1968), *Britain's Energy Supply*.
3. See *The Exploitation of North Sea Gas*, pp. 143–50.

The great debate on the 'right' output for coal which dominated Coal Board thinking in 1968/69 soon petered out. The years 1969/70 to 1971/72 brought new problems and developments. Particularly important was that serious coal shortages developed. Undistributed coal stocks, which stood at the very high level of 24·9 million tons in March 1969, fell to 6·2 million tons in March 1971. The supply situation in the winter of 1970/71 was critical and steps were taken to ease the position by allowing the conversion of some power stations to other fuels. In addition, the industry slowed down its colliery closure programme such that only nineteen pits were closed in 1969/70 and six in 1970/71, and most of these were exhausted. The labour rundown was negligible and indeed a quite major recruitment drive was mounted.

It would be quite wrong, however, to think that these trends represented the end of coal's decline. In fact, coal consumption fell by a massive 11·3 million tons between 1969/70 and 1970/71 (to 151·3 million tons) as serious a fall as any over the post-war period. The main explanation for the industry's seeming change of fortune was in productivity growth rather than demand conditions. In 1969/70 output per manshift was 43·4 cwt, only 0·9 cwt above the 1968/69 level, while 1970/71 saw an increase of 0·8 cwt and it is this which largely explains the slower rundown of the labour force and the need to eat into stocks.

The financial year 1971/72 was traumatic for the industry. In support of a substantial wage claim and following an over-time ban, a national coal strike was called in early 1972. Coal stocks were soon seriously depleted, or immobilised by picketing, and temporary fuel rationing was introduced. The dispute was settled by the Wilberforce inquiry whose, back-dated, award was expected to cost £100 million in a full year – equal to about one-third of the 1970/71 wage bill. Before the dispute the NCB was expecting to break even in 1971/72. The overtime ban and strike cost some £90 million and the wage increase about £50 million during 1971/72. These and other costs associated with getting production back to normal led to a deficit of £157 million in 1971/72. In March 1972 the

Government gave the industry a £100 million grant and the effective deficit was thereby reduced to £57 million. It was also agreed in March 1972 that coal prices should rise across the board by 7½ per cent perhaps giving £60 million in a full year.

Soon after the settlement the Government started a review of the industry's long term financial needs, and in December 1972 introduced a bill which reflected its deliberations. The bill proposed, first that £475 million should be written off the NCB's liabilities, so reducing the annual interest and depreciation charges by between £35 and £40 million. Secondly, it proposed some £500 million in grants over the period up to 1976 in order to control the industry's decline and/or to compensate it for some of the consequences of any rundown. In many ways the policies under this head are similar to earlier policies. A scheme to encourage early retirement is continued, as are schemes to compensate the Board for the costs of colliery closures and redundancy payments. The earlier scheme to encourage coal consumption by the electricity industry is continued though in a slightly different form. Some £210 million has been allocated to limit pit closures in the Development Areas, again not a new policy though the funds available are large by earlier standards. A new direction is that funds are available to subsidise coal stocks held by the NCB – presumably to encourage the use of stocks as temporary alternatives to rapid manpower rundown.

By the end of 1972 the Government, through the capital write off, had put the industry on a much more sound financial footing. At the same time it had secured powers which could be used to slow down the industry's decline. The extent to which it has to use these powers will depend on the industry's productivity performance and its ability to stop the decline in its markets.

5 The Railway Industry

The four companies making up the pre-war railway industry were nationalized on 1 January 1948. British Railways became a subsidiary of the British Transport Commission, a body which also had responsibility for other parts of the nationalized transport sector, and this structure remained until 1963 when the British Railways Board, a separate public corporation, took over responsibility for the industry. In 1948 the State took over an industry which had five basic historical characteristics. Firstly, the industry had grown up largely in the Victorian period and indeed the greater part of the system was established before 1870. Secondly, the railway companies had never made great profits, giving an average return on capital of about 4 per cent between 1870 and 1913 and only half that rate in the 1930s. Thirdly, the industry had been declining in terms of traffic carried even in the inter-war period – a result of the general economic troubles of the period plus growing competition from road transport. Fourthly, the industry was in need of new investment. The inter-war period had seen little railway modernization or investment because of the financial difficulties of the railway companies, while the Second World War saw the railways pushed almost to breaking point as a result of heavy traffic, and again there was negligible new or replacement investment. The arrears had not been made good by 1948 or indeed even by 1953.[1] Finally, the State took over an industry which had always been subject to considerable public control in its pricing and commercial policy generally.

The historical development of the railways is a fascinating

1. British Transport Commission, *Annual Report 1953*.

story but space limits us to considering the industry after nationalization.[1] This chapter gives a picture of the development of the railway industry after nationalization, its problems and the railway policies pursued. Section 1 discusses the size of the industry and its importance in the transport sector over the post-war period. Section 2 looks at the basic economic problems of railways. Section 3 traces railway policy to 1963 and the Beeching Report. Section 4 concludes the chapter with a discussion of post-Beeching railway problems and policies.

1. The Railway Industry: Its Size and Importance in the Transport Sector

A short description of the British railway industry in 1967 would conclude that it was a big industry but declining, that it secured most of its revenue from the carriage of freight and long-distance passengers, that it was an important part of the British transport system but played a smaller role than previously, and that it was an industry which was operated at a large and growing deficit. This section explains in more detail these aspects of the industry.

Some indicators of the size of the industry are shown in Table 17, which illustrates its decline in terms of staff and equipment relative to the early post-war period. Even so, by any standards it was in 1967 still a big industry. The size of its labour force made it one of the largest British employers, its turnover was over £400 million per annum, and investment averaged more than £100 million per annum throughout the 1960s.

About 60 per cent of the industry's receipts in 1967 came from the carriage of freight, much of this from the carriage of coal and coke (35 per cent) and iron and steel (13 per cent). On the passenger side, about 56 per cent of its revenue came from long-haul traffic. Stopping trains and suburban services accounted for the remainder.

1. For a concise history of the industry before nationalization see Savage, C. I. (1966), *An Economic History of Transport*, Hutchinson.

Table 17
Some Indicators of the Size of the Railway Industry: 1950
and 1967

	1950	1967	Index 1950 = 100
Gross receipts (£ million)	351·3	438·7	124·8
Working expenses (£ million)	326·1	536·1	164·4
Net receipts (£ million)	+25·2	−90·4	—
Railway staff (thousands)	606	318	52·5
Route miles*	19,471	13,172	67·7
Stations*	8487	3498	41·2
Locomotives*	19,741	5445	27·6
Passenger waggons*	42,218	20,787	49·2
Freight waggons*	1,107,225	466,623	42·1

Note: *Denotes end-of-year figures.
Sources: British Transport Commission, *Annual Report 1950*.
British Railways Board, *Annual Report 1967*.

Although the railways in 1967 still represented an important component of the British transport system, they were less important than previously. Table 18 illustrates this.

In 1967 about 11 per cent of freight tonnage transported in Britain went by rail, and reflecting the longer average rail hauls, about 18 per cent of freight ton-miles. For some heavy industries, the railways remained the major transport mode. About two-thirds of iron ore and steel scrap tonnage was carried by rail, as was the same proportion of coal and coke in bulk distribution. Two categories of heavy traffic, iron and steel, and coal and coke, accounted for about 75 per cent of total railway freight tons carried: as well as rail haulage being important to the heavy industries, their custom was important to the railways.

The industry was a less important carrier of passenger transport than it was for freight, for it accounted for a little less than 10 per cent of land passenger movements. It was

Table 18
Rail's Importance in the British Transport System

	1956	1961	1967
Land passenger mileage (thousand million)			
Bus, coach and tram	48·6	43·1	34·8
Private transport	59·5	97·7	165·2
Rail	24·5	24·1	21·1
Rail as a percentage of total	18·3	14·6	9·5
Freight (million tons)			
Road	993	1240	1500
Rail	277	238	201
Other[1]	56	61	86
Rail as a percentage of total	20·9	15·5	11·2
Freight (thousand million ton-miles)			
Road	23·2	32·3	43·0
Rail	21·5	17·6	13·6
Other	10·2	10·6	16·6
Rail as a percentage of total	39·2	29·1	18·4

Note: 1. This covers coastal shipping, inland waterways and
pipelines. The rapid growth of this group has largely arisen
out of the growth of pipelines which carried 2 million tons in
1956 and 27 million tons in 1967. Inland waterway freight
was 20 million tons in 1956 and 7 million tons in 1967.
Coastal shipping was 44 million tons and 52 million tons in
1956 and 1967 respectively.
Source: Central Statistical Office, *Annual Abstract of Statistics
1967*, p.200.

only half as important as the bus and motor coach industry,
while passenger mileage by private transport was eight times
as great as that on the railways. However, the industry has a
more important role in long-distance passenger travel than
these figures would suggest, since a high proportion of private
transport mileage is very short-distance. Table 18 above shows
the falling traffic on the railways over the period 1956–67,
during which other transport modes, except public passenger

motor transport, were expanding. The inevitable result was a decline in the railways' importance in the transport sector.

The diminishing importance of the industry as freight and passenger carrier was a result of many factors but two major ones were, firstly, competition from other transport forms both for passengers and freight, and secondly, on the freight side, the decline or slow growth of those industries and sectors for which the railways were major carriers. It is not possible to quantify the importance of these two factors, but growth in the use of private vehicles is fairly obviously the major reason for the downturn in passenger activity, since bus and coach transport has fallen back even more rapidly than rail. The fall in the amount of freight going by rail is undoubtedly a result of competition from road and pipeline, but the run-down of the coal industry and relative stagnation in the iron and steel industry have also contributed. In 1956 the railways were carrying 168 million tons of coal and coke and only 122 million tons in 1967, and the greater part of this fall was a result of the diminished size of the coal industry rather than competition from alternative transport modes.

One of the most remarkable and disturbing aspects of British Railways' operations over the period up to 1968 was the rising working deficit. A small working surplus averaging about 7 per cent of total revenue up to 1953 fell to 4 per cent in 1954 and virtually disappeared in 1955, and from then onwards the industry suffered a growing deficit which by 1962 had reached £102 million. Although the 1967 working deficit of £90·5 million was below the 1962 figure, it amounted to about 22 per cent of total revenue. On top of the working deficit are interest charges. The small surpluses on working account were large enough to cover these up to 1953 but not after that date. The total deficit – working deficit plus interest charges – amounted in 1967 to £153 million, almost one-third of total revenue.

This large and growing deficit of British Railways was due in part to the two factors discussed above, namely the decline or slow growth of industries for which it was a major carrier, and secondly, the increasing competition from alternative transport modes, particularly road. But these were incidental rather than basic causes of the railways' financial difficulties. Declining industries may suffer a fall in business, but they can often reorganize their activities so that they do not necessarily suffer deficits, let alone continuing losses of the proportions experienced by British Railways. The main explanation of the persistent deficit lies in the fact that railway operations present a number of difficult economic problems – notably in costing and pricing and in meeting peak demand – and for a variety of reasons British Railways proved unable to develop adequate economic policies to deal with the worsening situation. The next section outlines in more detail the economic problems of the railways, and sections 3 and 4 discuss railway policy.

2. Basic Economic Problems of Railways

One of the main difficulties of railway operations is the identification and allocation of costs to particular services. The cost structure of railways and the costing principles used have been the subject of much discussion by transport economists in recent years, but here we can only outline the characteristics of costs. The simplest type of costs to allocate are those associated with the running of a particular service, e.g. the fuel used by the locomotive and the wages paid to the crew. These are direct and specific costs. The problem arises with indirect costs, which can be of three kinds. Firstly, there are general overhead costs of administration; secondly, there are the costs of manning stations and depots; and thirdly, and much the most important indirect costs, there are the track costs associated with a particular part of the route mileage. Track costs include the cost of providing and maintaining permanent way, and the cost of signalling. In respect of a particular train or service these costs are treated as being both fixed and joint. They are fixed in the sense that they must be incurred if any service is to be provided at all, and they are joint costs since they allow the running of additional trains or services at no additional cost (assuming some spare capacity in the system). The Beeching Report estimated that in 1961 the cost of maintaining and signalling the running track (excluding stations and sidings track) amounted to about one-quarter of the railways' total revenue. The Report commented that 'this is a fixed cost, in the full sense of the term, all the while the route system remains unchanged.'[1]

One of the main points of discussion among transport economists is whether indirect costs are in fact fixed costs as the economist views them. Are these costs indeed independent of traffic in the sense that the withdrawal of some or most services would leave these costs unchanged, or is there some proportion which is 'escapable' and varies, within limits, as traffic varies? We shall return to this question later, but the important point is that a high proportion of railway costs can be regarded as fixed in the short run. Over the system as a whole, track costs and administrative costs are fixed, whereas the direct costs of particular services are variable, in that they will not be incurred if the service is not run, though of course once it has been decided to run a particular service, its fuel and wage costs are again largely independent of the number of passengers or quantity of goods carried. For the over-all route system the high level of fixed costs means that the profitable operation of the railways demands a high density of traffic so that the fixed costs can be spread over a high level of output. In addition, the railway system should ideally have this high-density traffic spread evenly over the day and year, but in practice the industry is not so fortunate. Though parts of the railway route system do have regular high-density traffic, a major problem in railway operation is the existence of peak demand for passenger services at certain times of the day or year. These peak demands mean that the track and equipment provided to meet the peak lies idle for the remainder of the time, and the nature of the track costs incurred creates problems of allocating joint costs between services.

Enough has been said to indicate that the profitable running of the railway industry requires careful economic policies,

1. British Railways Board (1963), *The Reshaping of British Railways*, H.M.S.O., part 1, p.9.

and there are four main requirements. Firstly, all services should be costed as accurately as possible, with joint and fixed costs allocated between services as far as possible. Secondly, prices should be charged according to these costs though with allowance for competitive strategy. Thirdly, those services or parts of the system which are unprofitable and incapable of being made profitable by lowering costs or increasing prices, should be cut out. Fourthly, every attempt should be made to attract profitable traffic to the railways in order that the industry's fixed costs can be spread. The growing deficit of the 1950s and 1960s can be explained by the failure or inability to pursue in a sufficiently vigorous manner policies fulfilling these four requirements.

3. Railway Policy 1948–1963

Between nationalization in 1948 and the publication of the Beeching Report in 1963, we can pick out two main areas of policy for examination; firstly, the problem of devising an efficient pricing policy, and secondly, the attempt to stabilize unit costs and attract traffic by massive investment in modernization and reconstruction.

The setting of prices according to costs and competitive strategy is an important requirement for any industry but particularly the railways where there exist considerable differences in the costs of providing different services. The railways, up to 1962 and even beyond, did not enjoy complete freedom in their pricing policy.[1] Under the 1947 Transport Act, the British Transport Commission had to submit its charges structure to the Transport Tribunal which had the power to accept or reject proposals. This control of prices was not new. During the inter-war period and indeed up to 1953, the railways had the status of a 'common carrier', i.e. they were legally obliged to carry any traffic offered to them. They had to publish their rates and charges and were

1. For an excellent description of railway freight charges up to 1957, see Harrison, A. A. (1957), 'Railway freight charges', *Journal of the Institute of Transport*, vol. 27, pp.143–56.

forbidden to discriminate against any traffic or class of traffic. This made it easier for competitors to undercut railway rates. Under the 1947 Act, customers and competitors had the right to object before the Transport Tribunal to proposed charges, and in its decisions the Tribunal had to keep in mind the obligation of the Transport Commission to equate costs with revenue, taking one year with another. 'In practice however the phrase "taking one year with another" [was] interpreted very broadly by both the Tribunal and the Minister of Transport to justify postponing, modifying or even rejecting charges proposals despite current deficits.'[1]

The charging system actually in operation up to 1957 was largely based on value and distance for freight, and distance for passengers, with discounts for season-ticket holders. These charging methods did not at all reflect the cost of supplying particular services. For freight it meant that the railways were left with the low-value high-bulk traffic such as steel, coal, etc., and though the railways were better able to carry such traffic than the roads, it was not very profitable for them to do so. High-value low-bulk traffic went to the roads, though it would have been quite easy and profitable for the railways to carry. For passengers, the system was perverse, in that commuters who imposed high costs on the system actually paid less than the average tariff per mile. Also, little or no distinction was made between fares on stopping-train services and those on long-distance services, though the costs of providing these services were very different. Consequently there was a considerable degree of cross-subsidization between profitable and unprofitable services which gave competing transport modes the opportunity to cream off the more profitable traffic, with the railways being increasingly left with its less profitable services.

The 1953 Transport Act attempted to liberate the industry from these controls. It proposed that the Tribunal should have powers in deciding only on the maximum charges, and should allow the industry to charge as it felt fit below these maxima.

1. Gwilliam, K. M. (1964), *Transport and Public Policy*, Allen & Unwin, p.97.

The 1953 Act could not, however, be implemented until the British Transport Commission had provided a charging structure and level upon which the Tribunal could deliberate, and a series of delays by both the Commission and the Tribunal meant that it was not until July 1957 that the new scheme was operational. The new scheme largely kept passenger fares on the basis of distance, but for freight it developed a number of categories and proposed a maximum charging scheme based on costs of handling these groups. Below the maxima fixed by the Transport Tribunal, the Commission was free to fix its own charges which did not have to be published. Unfortunately, because of the delays, some of the maximum charges were fixed below the rates then being charged, so that the railways lost 'several million pounds of revenue per annum.'[1] Also, the maxima could only be changed with the consent of the Tribunal, and objections by interested parties still had to be heard.

By 1957, therefore, the railways had in principle much more freedom to vary charges than they had had before, but it was still qualified by the existence of the Transport Tribunal and the influence of the Minister of Transport who, in 1952 and 1956, had limited proposed tariff increases with a consequent loss of revenue to the industry. In practice, however, the power of the Commission to reduce cross-subsidization on the passenger side was severely limited, since this would have meant an increase in the maximum fares for certain types of traffic, and this required the permission of the Transport Tribunal. For freight traffic, though, the Commission was by 1960 attempting to relate prices to the cost of carriage.

The second broad area of policy in the 1950s was an attempt to make up for the neglect of the 1940s through a Modernization Plan which would reduce the cost of railway operations and improve the efficiency of service so as to attract more traffic. The Plan aimed specifically at improving track and signalling so as to give higher speeds, replacing steam locomotives by diesel or electric, modernizing passenger rolling

1. Select Committee on Nationalised Industries (1960), *British Railways*, H.M.S.O., p. 345.

stock, and remodelling and speeding up the freight services, partly by reducing the number of depots and installing continuous braking on freight waggons. The Plan was published in 1955 when the estimated cost was £1200 million over fifteen years, revised in 1957 to £1660 million. In spite of this vast capital expenditure, the Modernization Plan was not subject to detailed economic scrutiny. The Select Committee on Nationalised Industries, reporting in 1960, complained of 'laxity of financial control' (p. liii), and took as a detailed example the electrification of the London–Liverpool–Manchester line which accounted for over 10 per cent of the total investment. The Committee found that no prior calculation had been made of the rate of return to be expected, and *ex post* calculations indicated a rate of return of between 5 and 7 per cent, as against interest on capital of 5–6 per cent. In other words, if the scheme made any profit at all it was likely to be only marginal. The important point was that like many other parts of the Modernization Plan, costs and expected receipts had not been estimated, and that in the event, the contribution to the industry's financial solvency would be small, much less than the Commission's optimistic but unquantified hopes.

By 1960, it was becoming recognized that the financial problems of the railways were too serious to be solved by the Modernization Plan or piecemeal attempts to improve efficiency, for example through the better utilization of manpower. It was clear to the Select Committee that the railways had little idea of the real cost of most of their services, and that consequently the efficiency and profitability of these services were not known. In fact, the Permanent Secretary at the Ministry of Transport confessed that 'one of the most difficult things in the Ministry is to discover where money is being lost' (p. 270). The railways claimed that freight and commuter services were at least breaking even, long-distance passenger trains made a surplus, and the whole of the working deficit came from stopping-trains, though the Select Committee were not convinced of this. It was quite clear that a much more accurate costing of the various services was needed, and that once the whole system had been examined it must be remodelled, with the abandonment where possible of uneconomic services. Earlier reshaping had been *ad hoc* and small-scale: between 1950 and 1961 only 1600 miles of route were abandoned out of a total route mileage of 19,500 in 1950. In 1963 when the working deficit alone had reached £75 million, a plan was published which put forward proposals for remodelling the system. This, *The Reshaping of British Railways*, is better known as the Beeching Report.

The first detailed study of British Railways, it aimed at investigating and costing the various parts of the system, and it gave quantified confirmation of what was becoming increasingly obvious, that the system was too big and that many parts of it were so under-utilized that they were a long way from covering their costs, let alone making a profit. One-third of route mileage accounted for only one per cent of total rail passenger miles, and one-third (usually the same lines) carried only one per cent of total freight ton-miles. Half the route carried 4 per cent and 5 per cent of passenger miles and freight ton-miles respectively. The cost of this under-utilization was very high and 'half of the system earns far less than sufficient to cover the costs of providing route to permit movement with no allowance whatsoever for movement or other costs'.[1] Further examples of under-utilization were found with stations, depots and rolling stock. Half the stations and the same proportion of freight depots accounted for only 2 per cent and 3 per cent of total passenger and freight receipts respectively. About one-third of the freight waggons were considered surplus to requirements, while a similar proportion of passenger coaches were used less than eighteen times a year, mainly to accommodate peak holiday traffic.

The Report found not only that money was being lost on the low-density routes (mainly rural stopping services) but that considerable losses were being made by suburban services, particularly around London. The suburban services lost money because although they had very high density traffic at peak travelling times, the system was largely lying

1. *The Reshaping of British Railways*, part 1, p.10.

idle for the rest of the day.[1] Fares were so low and the incidence of fixed costs so high that suburban services were losing some £25 million in 1961.

In response to the findings, the Report proposed that a considerable number of lines, depots and stations be closed and that surplus waggons and carriages be scrapped, but it is wrong to see the policy of the Beeching Report as being purely a negative one of closures, service withdrawals and scrapping. On the suburban services, it recognized the need to maintain these from the viewpoint of the particular cities involved and recommended that fares be more closely aligned with costs, and its positive proposals also included plans for cutting costs through reduced documentation and increased standardization of equipment. One of its major proposals concerned the introduction and development of liner trains. Liner trains, which were to be an important part of railway freight policy in the following years, are regular fast through trains with permanently coupled waggons on which goods arrive and leave in containers. They have advantages for customers and the railways: for the customer, speed, reliability and freedom from pilferage; for the railways, lower costs through the reduced need for shunting, documentation and double handling. It was estimated that they would be competitive with road transport for distances of about 100 miles and highly competitive for greater distances. The railways, it was hoped, would be able to gain net revenues of £10–12 million per annum from the operation of this service by 1968.

From the mid-1950s up to 1963, when the Beeching Report appeared, the railways' deficit had continued to increase. This was not surprising, considering the circumstances in which the railways found themselves. The railways' unit costs were rising, while the heavy industries on which the railways

1. The Beeching Report discussing London's peak problem commented: 'The peak load, measured over half an hour, is about 10 times the average level over the hours from 6 a.m. to midnight, and 12 times the average over 24 hours. The route and rolling stock capacity provided to deal with the peak is used to only 10 per cent of its capacity during the hours over which it might normally be expected to carry passengers' (p.21).

depended for so much revenue were stagnating or declining. Competition from road was increasing and rail traffic falling, and since the route system was unchanged, the high fixed costs were being spread over less traffic. In addition, the unsuitable pricing system, with its elements of cross-subsidization, diminished the railways' competitiveness in those traffics which they could carry best and where greatest profits could be earned. The industry was caught in a vicious circle; rising costs, falling traffic, the rising incidence of fixed costs, the inability to recoup costs through price changes, and the tardy action in remodelling the system – all these made rising deficits inevitable.

The authors of the Beeching Report had high hopes for its effect on railway finances. The whole parcel of measures would, it was hoped, create conditions whereby 'much (though not all) of the Railway's deficit should be eliminated by 1970 but only if the proposals are implemented with vigour' (p. 54). The forecast turned out to be very optimistic, and the 1968 deficit was virtually as high as in 1962. The next section examines developments since 1963 to explain why the deficits were not reduced as had been hoped, and outlines future policy for the railways.

4. The Railways after Beeching

The Transport Act of 1962 gave control of the railways to the British Railways Board. To give the Board a better start in life, £705 million of the railways' accumulated debt to the Ministry of Transport (mainly made up by accrued losses) was put into suspense, and did not carry interest unless the Minister so decided: up to 1968 it was in fact non-interest bearing. In addition, the railways reassessed the book value of their assets, and the revised values were £312 million less than had appeared in the Transport Commission accounts. This was treated as a capital deficit, and was not at this stage written off. In spite of any encouragement received from these financial measures, the railways did not manage to reduce the deficit to any great extent after the Beeching proposals, though they were able to contain it until 1967. Table 19 shows receipts and expenses for the period 1963 to 1968.

Table 19
Railway Receipts and Expenses 1963–8 (£ million)

	Working expenses	Receipts[1]	Operating deficit	Over-all deficit[2]
1963	550	463	87	134
1964	542	468	73	121
1965	546	466	80	132
1966	542	464	78	135
1967	536	439	97	153
1968 (estimated)	530	430	100	157

Notes: 1. Excluding receipts from ancillary activities.
2. Includes interest charges and also results of British Rail's subsidiary activities.
Source: National Board for Prices and Incomes (1968), Report no. 72, *Proposed Increases by British Railways Board in Certain Country-Wide Fares and Charges*, H.M.S.O., Cmnd 3656, p. 5.

The inability of the industry to reduce its deficit, and the increases after 1966 were a result of two main factors, the same factors as affected the railways in the 1950s and early 1960s. Firstly, there was the continuing competition from other transport modes and the decline in the industry's main industrial customers; and secondly, there was the failure of the railways to reduce costs and increase revenue, partly through no fault of their own but also partly because of their inadequate policy. On the first point, the railways' share of total ton-mileage fell from 30·6 per cent in 1963 to 24·9 per cent in 1967.[1] British Railways passenger traffic fell from 19·2

1. National Board for Prices and Incomes (1968), Report no. 72, *Proposed Increases by British Railways Board in Certain Country-Wide Fares and Charges*, H.M.S.O., Cmnd 3656, p.26. Coal traffic fell from 7·8 thousand million net ton-miles in 1963 to 6·0 in 1967. Iron and steel traffic fell from 2·6 to 2·4 over the same period while other freight rose slightly from 5·0 to 5·2.

thousand million passenger-miles in 1963 to 18·1 in 1967, representing 11 per cent and less than 9 per cent of total passenger mileage respectively. This fall in traffic came about in spite of improved service through the introduction or extension of a number of schemes aimed at increasing speeds and attracting new traffic. These included straightening of track, extension of continuously welded rails, resiting of junctions and the introduction of automatic warning systems which give the driver an audible indication of the state of signals ahead. At the same time, the industry was extending its advertising and brightening up its stations and its 'image' generally in an attempt to attract more custom.

One side of the industry's attempt to reduce costs was the continuation of the reorganization schemes which had been instituted under the Modernization Plan. These included the replacement of steam by diesel and electric locomotives, the development of automatic level crossings, the extension of mechanized track maintenance, the concentration of traffic on fewer and more mechanized freight depots, the rapid extension of power signal boxes which increase the area controlled from a single box, and greater centralization of waggon control bringing a more economic use of freight rolling stock. Also on the freight side there was the introduction of merry-go-round trains (permanently coupled trains running between a colliery and power station), the extension of company trains and the completion by the end of 1967 of the freight liner train plan. The other major attempt to cut costs came from the reduction of plant and staff through the implementation of the Beeching proposals to cut out uneconomic services. Table 20 below gives some indication of the rundown of staff and plant between 1962 and 1967 as a result of cutting out uneconomic lines and the other measures to increase productivity.

The various cost-saving measures and the cut back in the size of the industry were not sufficient to stop costs per traffic unit rising, from 3·8d. (1·58p) in 1963 to 4·1d. (1·71p) in 1967.[1]

1. Prices and Incomes Board, Report no. 72. A traffic unit for freight is one net ton-mile; that for passengers is one passenger mile.

Competition from other transport modes plus inappropriate pricing policies meant that revenue per traffic unit only rose from 3·2d. (1·33p) in 1963 to 3·3d. (1·38p) in 1967. The rise in the deficit was inevitable.

Table 20
Staff and Equipment in British Railways:
End 1962 and End 1967 (thousands)

	1962	1967
Staff	475·2	318·1
Locomotives	12·6	5·4
Passenger coaching vehicles	33·6	20·8
Freight vehicles	862·6	466·6
Stations	6·7	3·5
Marshalling yards	0·8	0·2
Route miles	17·5	13·2
Track miles (including sidings)	47·4	36·5

Source: British Railways Board, *Annual Reports*.

The inability of the industry to hold back increases in unit costs and reduce the deficit was in part a result of factors largely beyond its control. Firstly, the industry was not able to make all the cuts in the system size which it desired or that were required under the Beeching proposals. Successive Ministers of Transport recognized that a commercially viable railway system was not politically acceptable or socially desirable. Route and station closures were thus much slower and less drastic than the railways proposed, and there was no compensation for the social obligations and costs that the railways were thereby forced to carry. Secondly, there were heavy union pressures for increased wages. The industry, not always under its own volition, succumbed to these pressures.[1]

1. The Cameron Report (1955), H.M.S.O., Cmd 9352, had stated that 'the employees of such a national service should receive a fair and adequate wage, and ... in broad terms, the railwayman should be in no worse case than his colleagues in comparable industry'. The doctrine

In spite of the considerable decline in the labour force, labour costs were almost as high in 1967 (£342 million) as they had been in 1963 (£344 million) and many of the cost savings were swallowed up by higher wages. Thirdly, the trade unions resisted some of the changes in manning which the railways proposed, on the grounds that the rundown of the industry was proceeding at too great a pace. Also, the development and growth of the freightliner services was held back by labour problems, and it was not until mid-1967 that the unions agreed to allow lorries other than those belonging to British Railways to use the freightliner terminals.

Though some of the causes of the continuing deficit were outside the railways' control, there were other areas where the industry's commercial and financial policy was deficient. The Beeching Report had been looked upon as a blueprint for salvation, but hindsight suggests that even the complete implementation of the Report would still have left the railways in a difficult financial position. As it was, there were various possibilities of cost-saving which were pursued less zealously than the critics of the railways would have liked, for example the simplification of timetabling, the development of un-staffed stations, and most important, the reduction of track costs. The railways regarded track costs as fixed and indepen-dent of traffic, but this is true in only a limited sense, since the standard of maintenance and signalling on a track de-pends on the type and density of traffic. Some critics have maintained that the average level of maintenance of British Railways' track is too high, and that a 'downgrading' of substantial portions of the route system would be possible, with consequent savings in track costs.[1] Another possibility is single-tracking (common in many European countries) which can be made to carry remarkably high traffic densities.

---

of comparability was enshrined in the Guillebaud Report of 1960, and it continued to be the main criterion used by the trade unions up to 1968.

1. See for example Joy, S. (1964), 'Railway track costs', *Journal of Industrial Economics*, vol. 13, pp. 74–89; reprinted in Munby, D. (ed.) (1968). *Transport*, Penguin Books.

Single-tracking would cut costs, since the cost of maintaining and signalling single tracks is about 60 per cent of the cost of double tracks.[1]

However, a major criticism of British Railways was again of its pricing policy. The Transport Act 1962 belatedly recognized that the railways should have greater freedom to fix their own tariffs, but the industry does not seem to have used this freedom to charge according to costs and competitive strategy. In part this was due to the old problem of lack of knowledge of the costs attributable to particular services, but the Prices and Incomes Board Report pointed out that the railways also had little idea of the effect of tariff increases on revenue, and that there was an over-concentration on general increases. The Report commented:

The marketing information available is, however, so sparse that it is not certain that all the proposals for fares and charges increases will, in fact, increase net revenue. It would seem to us that in the past, British Rail has tended to sell, and sell unprofitably, the service traditionally provided rather than adjust the service to what can be economically sold. General increases in fares and charges have diminished total traffics, and increased unit costs, the increase leading to increased fares, with each turn of the screw aggravating the problem ... we are disposed to be sceptical of the value of standard increases, and to attach greater importance to the need to particularise, in other words to increase net revenue by pricing more flexibly in line with particular marketing possibilities, even granted that the information available for doing this is limited (p.20).

This amounts to a comprehensive and justified criticism of the whole of British Railways' commercial strategy.

By 1967, then, the railways were still in serious financial difficulties. Estimates for that year, shown in Table 21, were that all classes of traffic made a loss.

1. Estimates of route costs by number of tracks can be found in *The Reshaping of British Railways*, p.9. The possibility and benefits of single-tracking were considered by Joy and Foster in a paper given to the Institute of Civil Engineers in mid-1967. A report and comment is in the *Economist*, 29 July 1967.

Table 21
Analysis of Revenue and Costs by Type of Traffic 1967 (£m)

Type		Receipts	Deficit on total cost
Passenger:	Fast/semi-fast	102	19
	Stopping	28	42
	Suburban	53	24
Total passenger		183	85
Passenger parcels, etc.		55	6
Freight:	Coal	91	11
	Iron and steel	32	15
	Other	56	40
	Sundries	22	26
Total freight		201	92

Source: British Railways Board, *Annual Report 1967*, Appendix 1.

Total costs include interest and depreciation, and it is acknowledged that the apportionment of joint and indirect costs may be imprecise. The important point, though, is that all classes of traffic contributed to the over-all losses, and indeed only fast/semi-fast passenger traffic and coal traffic showed substantial surpluses over *direct* costs, while for suburban services and passenger parcels, gross receipts were slightly above direct costs. Obviously, a further substantial reduction in the railways' deficit was unlikely without major policy changes. The basis for these was laid with the publication of the White Paper on *Railway Policy* in November 1967[1] and the subsequent Transport Act 1968 which gave legislative effect to the proposals.

Four major changes were foreshadowed which would make an immediate contribution to the reduction of the railways'

1. Ministry of Transport (1967), *Railway Policy*, H.M.S.O., Cmnd 3439.

deficit in 1969.[1] Firstly, there would be a capital reconstruction under which the £705 million of suspended debt and an additional £557 million of interest-bearing debt would be wiped out. The immediate effect was to relieve the British Railways Board of the whole of the industry's accumulated losses, and the capital assets were written down 'to a level at which it is reasonable to expect that interest payments can be met out of revenue early in the 1970s'.[2] It was estimated that in 1969 the capital reconstruction would reduce the railways' interest payments by £30 million and depreciation charges by £20 million.

Secondly, sundries traffic was transferred to National Carriers Ltd, a wholly owned subsidiary of the National Freight Corporation. A subsidy of up to £60 million has been given to meet initial losses over the first five years of National Carriers Ltd operations. The immediate gain to the railways' account in 1969 was £20 million.

Thirdly, a new arrangement was devised for unremunerative passenger services. The Minister of Transport might decide that certain services should be continued 'on broad social and economic grounds', even though they were not covering costs and the railways would have preferred to withdraw the services entirely. In such cases the Minister and the British Railways Board were to agree on the service to be provided and on the level of specific grants to be made to the railways as compensation for continuing to run each uneconomic service. In 1969/70 these grants totalled £57·5 million.

Fourthly, the White Paper recognized that the rundown of the railways had left the Board with 'surplus capacity' in its track and signalling equipment, and it was decided to give the railways a grant to eliminate this surplus over the period up to 1974. The maximum paid out over the five years is expected to be £50 million, with £17 million being paid in 1969/70.

This extensive financial reconstruction was intended to put the railways into such a position that they would break even

1. For details of these proposals, see *Railway Policy*, and the Prices and Incomes Board, Report no. 72, pp. 8–11.
2. *Railway Policy*, p.5.

by about 1974, and in 1969 the railways' total financial benefit from these measures was estimated to be about £140 million. However, the Prices and Incomes Board calculated that on the basis of the 1967 fares and charges structure the railways would still lose at least £13 million, and probably more if proper provision were made for asset renewal and general reserves.[1] It is most important to realise that this virtual elimination of the railways' deficit in 1969 was entirely due to accounting changes. Almost £80 million of the deficit still existed but had been removed from the railways' accounts: £20 million went to National Carriers Ltd, while £58 million was paid by the taxpayer through the Ministry of Transport's subsidy grants instead of appearing as a loss in British Railways' accounts. Furthermore, the financial measures did not in themselves lead to any improvement in the railways' efficiency, except insofar as they might improve morale: the White Paper commented that

it is clearly impossible to expect the management and the men of this great industry to continue to try to do their jobs under the demoralising shadow of this immense deficit (p. 5).

The White Paper estimated that the railways would break even by about 1974, and one of the major problems was that the revenue forecasts it made were incorrect, especially for freight traffic. The estimates were based on a 3 per cent per annum growth of output and 3·3 per cent per annum growth of industrial production. Obviously a slower rate of industrial expansion, especially in heavy industry, has completely upset the railways' estimates of future revenue. Also, the White Paper appears to have made no allowance for technological change in road transport and the extension of the motorway network which favours long-distance road haulage; road transport may well be more competitive than the White Paper allowed. For one thing, the system of quantity licensing was not introduced as the Transport Act had suggested. This system had been designed to direct more freight on to the railways by requiring special authorization for

1. Prices and Incomes Board, Report no. 72, pp. 8–11.

freight travelling over 100 miles in lorries of over 16 tons weight. Road transport has therefore continued to take a larger share of the growth in freight traffic.

Another area where the railways have done less well than expected is in the freightliner services. The 1967 estimates of freightliner traffic 'in the early 1970s' were 4500 million ton-miles, as against the Beeching Report's 1973 estimate of 6440 million ton-miles (p. 43). In 1971 the revenue from freight-liners was £6·2 million, compared with total freight revenue of £193·1 million, and the service made no contribution to British Rail's operating profit. It would appear that earlier estimates underestimated the distance at which rail begins to have an advantage over road. The Beeching Report thought that this 'break-even' distance was about 100 miles, and that above this distance rail costs would be below road haulage costs. By the end of the 1960s, it seemed that the break-even point was at least 150 miles, and in the important area of 100–150 mile hauls, competition from road hauliers was especially fierce.

The railways' problem at the start of the 1970s was to improve efficiency and productivity. Technical efficiency should continue to improve as a result of the modernization and closure programme and from improvements in track, signalling and equipment. Between 1962 and 1971 the railways had cut route mileage from 17,500 to about 11,650. They had about 3,800 locomotives compared with 12,600 in 1962, and staff had been reduced from 475,200 to about 201,700. Further technical advances can be foreseen. The new High Speed Train and, in the mid 1970s, the Advanced Passenger Train will help attract long-distance passenger traffic, while continuous attempts are being made to improve the quality and reliability of freight service. However, the key problem for the railways is whether they can stabilize and reduce costs, and here prospects are not so bright.

The railways are still very labour intensive and in 1971 staff costs (wages, salaries and related costs) accounted for 62 per cent of rail operating expenditure. This makes it difficult for them to avoid increases in unit costs in an inflationary situation such as 1970/71, and the benefits of the railways' productivity negotiations in the late 1960s have since been swallowed up by rising staff costs. In 1971, for example, cost savings of £20 million were made, but operating expenses still rose by £46 million. The profit before interest was £30·2 million, and the overall result was a loss of £15·4 million. This takes into account grants from the Government, of £63 million in respect of unremunerative services and of £27 million as special assistance to compensate the railways for complying with the Government's price restraint policy.

The past experience of the railways does not make for optimism over their prospects for the 1960s. The Transport Act gave them a favourable administrative and financial framework within which to operate, and the railways' commercial policies are now more soundly based. But this is not enough. A small country with a slowly growing economy and inflationary tendencies is a poor environment for railway operations, and it may be significant that in 1972 there were persistent rumours of further cuts in the railways network.

6 The Nationalized Road Haulage Industry

The road haulage industry has been of increasing importance in the carriage of freight within Britain. As the railways declined so the proportion of goods going by road increased, and in 1971 85 per cent of goods tonnage and 63 per cent of goods ton-miles went by road.[1] However, the nationalized road haulage sector is unlike other public corporations in that it has only a minority share of the total market for carriage of goods by road: there are a large number of private road hauliers operating in competition with the nationalized industry, and an even larger number of 'own-account' carriers running vehicles solely to carry their own goods. The diversity of the industry therefore means that the problems of road haulage as a whole do not necessarily emerge from a consideration only of the nationalized concerns, and we must constantly compare the respects in which the publicly-owned businesses differ from the others. The year 1968 represented a watershed for road transport, since the Transport Act 1968 completely changed the framework within which the whole industry operated and set up a new structure of administration and control for the nationalized undertakings.

This chapter has three sections. Section 1 traces briefly the development of the regulatory framework within which the industry operated up to 1968. Though this has now been superseded by the Transport Act 1968, it is essential to an understanding of nationalized road haulage. Section 2 deals with the progress of the nationalized undertakings over the period 1963/8 in relation to the rest of the industry. During these

1. *Annual Abstract of Statistics* (1972), Table 241.

years, nationalized road haulage was under the control of the Transport Holding Company which was one of the most successful public corporations and which operated in rather an unusual way. Finally, section 3 outlines the provisions of the Transport Act 1968 which deal with road haulage, and assesses their likely impact on the road haulage industry in general and the nationalized sector in particular.

1. Licensing and Nationalization

The licensing system as it was in 1967 had changed only in detail from the system laid down in the early 1930s. Before 1930 there were few limitations on road haulage vehicles, and entry to the industry was easy since the minimum capital required (one vehicle) was small. The result was a very rapid growth of small-scale road haulage enterprises during the 1920s, and this was accompanied by fierce competition for traffic. There were two reasons why these developments were, by 1930, causing some concern. Firstly, there was the view that the industry was undergoing wasteful and uneconomic competition and that 'in the interest of safety and amenity, some controls would have to be imposed'[1] Secondly, the railways were at that time very tightly regulated (e.g. they had 'common carrier' obligations and had to publish all rates and charges), and were being badly hit by the flexible and unregulated competition from road. Following the Royal Commission on Transport 1928 and the Salter Conference 1932, the basic system of licensing was established by the Road and Rail Traffic Act 1933.

This Act provided for three types of vehicle licence. The 'A' licence applied to vehicles being used for the general carriage of goods for hire and reward; the 'B' licence applied to vehicles used both for carriage for hire and reward, and

1. Ministry of Transport (1965), *Report of the Committee on Carriers' Licensing*, H.M.S.O., p. 9. This Report, usually called the Geddes Report, contains a useful short summary of licensing procedures up to 1965.

for carriage of the operator's own goods; and 'C' licences were issued for vehicles which were to be used only to carry the operator's own goods. C licences were normally issued on request but A and B licences had to be obtained from licensing authorities, and they would only be granted if existing capacity was unable to meet demand. The applicant had to prove the need for a new service, while existing operators and the railways could, and did, enter objections on the grounds that sufficient capacity already existed. This licensing system continued up to 1939 and remained essentially unchanged until 1968. Its provisions obviously had a considerable effect on the development of road haulage, for the system favoured existing operators and made entry to the industry difficult, especially since the licensing authorities had to be assured of the applicant's ability to meet the provisions regarding safety, wages and working conditions and record-keeping. The declared objectives of licensing were to increase safety and to improve the competitive position of the railways by preventing unrestricted competition from the road hauliers. However, there is little evidence that the licensing system had much effect during the 1930s in fulfilling these objectives. It is true that the industry's safety record improved after licensing, but the Geddes Committee made the point that this was not necessarily because of the licensing procedure, and the safety record of private cars also improved over the same period. Furthermore, licensing appeared to have little effect in protecting the railways from 'unfair competition.' The railways continued to lose traffic to the road hauliers, and the railway companies themselves began to enter the road transport industry as a defensive measure and to deliver goods from the railheads. By 1939 the railway companies were among the largest operators of road haulage vehicles.

After the war, the Transport Act 1947 set up the British Transport Commission (B.T.C.) which was charged with providing 'an efficient, adequate, economical and properly integrated system of public inland transport and port facilities'. The main reason for nationalization was the desire to have an integrated transport policy and to eliminate wasteful competition by road and rail for the available traffic. Long-distance road haulage was therefore nationalized and all enterprises whose major business involved carriage of goods over 40 miles were taken over by the B.T.C., to form British Road Services (B.R.S.). C licence vehicle fleets were not nationalized and traders could therefore continue to carry own-account traffic. Short-distance A and B licence-holders could also continue in operation, though they were forbidden to operate more than 25 miles from their bases without a special permit. From 1948, when the acquisition of private fleets began, the Road Transport Executive of the B.T.C. (later the Road Haulage Executive) faced several difficult problems, most of them reflecting the organizational and operational structure of the industry and of the firms it had acquired.

First of all, there was the sheer size of the process of acquisition. The Road Transport Executive, of which B.R.S. was the operating arm, had to take over 3744 separate undertakings with a total vehicle fleet of some 42,000 lorries. This took until 1952 (though most large firms had been acquired by 1950), partly because 87 per cent of transactions required the full legal machinery of compulsory purchase. Secondly, a decision had to be taken on how the industry should be organized. It was difficult to see how the large number of small firms could be welded into an effective administrative structure, and in contrast to the previously decentralized nature of the industry, the Road Transport Executive set up a three-tier system of control, with divisions, districts and groups; it was not until 1951 that a two-tier system of divisions and districts was adopted with each division being a self-contained entity of about 1000 vehicles. Thirdly, immediately after nationalization, competition from C licence vehicles was much greater than had been expected. The number of C licences rose from 487,200 in 1947 to 590,526 in 1948 and 796,400 in 1951.[1] Also, the number of C licence vehicles of five tons and over more than doubled from 1948 to 1951, from 4800 to 11,088, which suggests that C licence-holders

1. *Annual Abstract of Statistics* (1948 and 1951).

were increasing their long-distance operations. Fourthly, the permit system for private A and B licence-holders did not begin operation until 1950, and even after that it was subject to wide and almost unchecked abuse, with supposedly short-distance operators carrying goods outside the 25 mile limit.[1] Finally, the consolidation of the enormous variety of pre-nationalization charging systems into a national schedule of road haulage rates was never achieved, and in the years up to 1952 charges were substantially based on pre-nationalization schedules.[2]

Apart from these problems on the road haulage side, the Transport Act 1947 did not achieve its aim of integrating road and rail transport. The British Transport Commission proved unable to deal with the vast number of administrative and economic problems involved in its statutory responsibilities. The B.T.C. was largely preoccupied by the problems of the railways, which had continuing difficulties throughout the post-war period. In 1952 the Conservative Government proposed denationalization of the major part of the road transport industry, and this came about in the Transport Act 1953. The intention was to dispose of most of British Road Services' vehicles, leaving B.R.S. with only that number which the pre-nationalization railway companies had owned. In the event, the disposal of trunk haulage vehicles proved very difficult, and in 1956 it was acknowledged that B.R.S. would have to keep the trunk services if they were to be maintained as an entity. Legislation to this effect meant that in 1956 B.R.S. remained by far the largest operator in the industry, with about 16,000 vehicles, 7000 of them for trunk haulage. B.R.S. also maintained the parcels service as a whole, for it was realized that this, like the trunk haulage service, would be more efficient if maintained as an entity.

The next substantial change came with the Transport Act 1962 which further decentralized the nationalized transport sector. The British Transport Commission was dissolved and

1. British Transport Commission, *Annual Report, 1952*, p. 94.
2. K. M. Gwilliam, *Transport and Public Policy*, p. 99.

its road haulage operations transferred to a new body, the Transport Holding Company (T.H.C.), from 1 January 1963. As its name suggests, this body exercised a rather different type of control over the nationalized road haulage units than had its predecessors. It worked through a structure of subsidiary companies (see section 2) and was enjoined to run them as in a commercial enterprise. The T.H.C.'s first Annual Report made the following point.

The use of a company-structure of a commercial character, as opposed to a single or monolithic structure, makes possible a much greater flexibility of organisation and also brings other advantages which the Holding Company has been careful not to throw away (p.4).

As well as road haulage companies, the T.H.C. controlled publicly-owned road passenger transport, shipping, travel and tourism and some manufacturing interests.

The operation of the road haulage sector of the Transport Holding Company is discussed in section 2, but two other important developments during the 1960s must be mentioned here. First, there was the Report of the Committee on Carrier Licensing (the Geddes Report), published in 1963. After studying the licensing system, the Geddes Committee concluded that licensing had signally failed to achieve the objectives often claimed for it. In particular, it had had no effect on safety or amenity, and probably had a deleterious effect on the industry's efficiency. The operation of the system had become unduly legalistic and was hedged around by case law, so that A and B licences were normally very difficult to obtain and entry to the industry was thereby strictly controlled. Also, the restriction of C licence-holders to own-account carriage tended to mean a lower utilization of C licence vehicles, mainly because such vehicles tended to run empty (e.g. on returning to their home bases) more often than A or B licence vehicles. In addition, the Committee believed that the licensing system had had no effect in diverting traffic towards the railways or changing the relative competitive position of road and rail. Their over-all conclusion was therefore that the whole licensing system should be abolished. Competition between enterprises would mean a more efficient industry, and stringent safety regulations could be applied to prevent competition having a bad effect on safety.

The second important development during the 1960s was the Transport Act 1968. In a sense this had its origins in the Geddes Report, for the Committee's condemnation of the licensing system was accepted by the Labour Government. But the Government decided that the proper course was not to abolish the licensing system entirely, but rather to revise the system so that the objectives of safety and road-rail co-ordination could be achieved. This revision came in the Transport Act 1968 which completely changed the structure of licensing and control of road haulage in an attempt to achieve a co-ordinated and integrated freight policy. We shall examine its likely effect in section 3.

2. Nationalized Road Haulage 1963–1968

When the Transport Holding Company took over the assets of British Road Services in 1963, it continued in a more explicit form the decentralization policy which the British Transport Commission had followed since 1953. The Transport Holding Company initially organized road haulage activities into three groups, each with a number of associated companies. The individual companies were in control of their own operations and were separately accountable to the Transport Holding Company. Common services and co-ordination of policies were provided by the British Road Services Federation whose responsibilities included wages and conditions of employment, training, technical and market research, and centralized buying. Table 22 shows the groupings with the number of subsidiary companies and the number of vehicles operated in 1963 and 1967, and 1967 employment.

In 1964 the Labour Government reversed the Conservatives' policy of not allowing the acquisition of new businesses. The T.H.C. then began to acquire other road haulage companies, and by 1967 the T.H.C. had 1900 more vehicles than in 1963.[1] The significant point, however, is that the T.H.C.'s road haulage interests were on average much larger than almost all other privately-owned companies in the industry. For convenience, we can group these interests together under the label British Road Services, though many other trade names existed, e.g. Pickfords, Tayforth, Harold Wood and Co.

Table 22
Road Haulage Interests of the Transport Holding Company

Groupings	Companies		Vehicles		Employment
	1963	1967	1963	1967	1967
General grouping	6	10	10,400	10,300	16,600
Parcels grouping	2	4	4100	4100	11,700
Pickfords grouping (specialist haulage)	3	7	1800	1600	4500
Tayforth grouping	—	32	—	1600	5300
Others	—		—	600	
Total	11	53	16,300	18,200	38,100

Source: T.H.C., *Annual Reports*, 1963 and 1967.

In its size, B.R.S. was quite untypical of the road haulage industry as a whole. In 1963, the last year for which data exist, half the operators in the industry had only one vehicle. Table 23 shows a detailed breakdown by size of fleet for A and B licence-holders, and includes the nationalized undertakings. Of the 29,000 vehicles in the largest fleet size-category, over 16,000 belonged to B.R.S. and another 8000 to British Railways. It is unlikely that the proportions of vehicles and

1. The T.H.C. also expanded into other sectors of business, and acquired some manufacturing interests.

Table 23

Operators and Vehicles by Size of Fleet, 1963

No. of vehicles	Operators		Vehicles	
	Number	Per cent	Number	Per cent
1	23,130	50·0	23,130	12·0
2–5	16,000	34·5	45,970	22·0
6–50	6940	15·0	90,900	44·0
51–100	160	0·4	10,100	5·0
101–200	33	} 0·1	6600	3·0
Over 200	17		28,900	14·0
Total	46,280	100·0	205,600	100·0

Source: National Board for Prices and Incomes (1965), Report no. 1, *Road Haulage Rates*, H.M.S.O., Cmnd 2695, p. 21.

operators changed very much in the period up to 1967.[1] Of course, Table 23 shows only the vehicles and operators engaged in public haulage on A and B licences. There were in addition about 1¼ million vehicles with C licences which carried own-account traffic only. These were not in direct competition with B.R.S. in the public haulage market, though many C licence fleets were in fact used for long-distance traffic. As well as being very much larger than other firms in the industry, B.R.S. also had a different pattern of operations. B.R.S.'s main interest was in general haulage which accounted in 1967 for two-thirds of its vehicle mileage, with a particular specialization in long-distance haulage. As a result, its average length of haul was much higher than the average for the industry. In 1962 only 7 per cent of all licensed vehicle journeys and 8 per cent of those by A and B licensed vehicles were of

1. In terms of turnover, B.R.S. represented in 1967 about 3¼ per cent of the total road haulage industry and about 15 per cent of the commercial road haulage sector. These estimates indicate that B.R.S. was more important than a simple comparison based on vehicle numbers would indicate.

100 miles and over, while in 1967 47 per cent of B.R.S. general haulage journeys were of more than 100 miles.

To deal with B.R.S. as a whole in the context of the industry is to some extent misleading. B.R.S. was far from being a monolithic giant. The various groupings each had a number of subsidiary companies, each of them commercially responsible to the Transport Holding Company for the operation of its business, and these companies were by no means dominant in the sectors of industry to which they belonged. Indeed the T.H.C. in its first *Annual Report* in 1963 suggested that 'the Holding Company and its underlying limited companies should not, therefore, be thought of as "a nationalised industry" – a point of some consequence'.[1] In 1967 the decentralized method of control was acclaimed for its 'freedom and flexibility throughout the organisation as a whole, the resulting accountability and discipline, and the element of protection afforded against the more direct forms of abuse of public ownership'.[2] Obviously the T.H.C. was an unusual form of public corporation! Another point is that the B.R.S. companies were specialized by function, with particular companies within groupings concentrating on certain types of traffic, e.g. bulk liquids, abnormal loads, and contract hire. Thus B.R.S. was decentralized in management and control to a much greater extent than the over-all data might suggest, but the average B.R.S. company was still much larger than those in the private sector.[3]

The structure of the road haulage industry as a whole suggests two main questions. Firstly, what allowed the survival of so many small units, and secondly, how did the large organization of B.R.S. fit into the industry? The importance and prevalence of the small operator seem to be explained by a combination of economic and managerial factors. One point is that little capital is required to enter the industry as a one- or two-vehicle operator, though before 1968 an A or B

1. Transport Holding Company, *Annual Report 1963*, p.4.
2. ibid., p.3.
3. B.R.S. has never published data on tonnage carried or ton-miles performed, which makes precise comparisons impossible.

licence had to be obtained first. The vehicle licensing system
also had some effect in freezing the industrial structure, since
it was difficult for existing operators to expand or large new
operators to enter, so that the survival of small operators was
easier. Once in business, most small operators serve a localized
market or even a specialized sector of a local market, e.g.
transporting only coal or livestock. The 1962 Survey of Road
Transport showed that about 74 per cent of loaded end-to-
end journeys by *all* A and B licensed vehicles were of less than
25 miles, and most of these journeys would be by small operators. Another advantage for the owner of a small fleet is that
he can escape some overhead costs which a larger firm would
face, such as depots, engineering and maintenance, and
management. Insofar as he serves a local market the small
operator will tend to have good market information based on
personal contact, judgement and goodwill. The detailed administrative control which the small operator is able to exert
over his fleet will make possible a flexibility of response to
market pressures, and a competitive pricing and supply
strategy which may be difficult for the large firm to achieve.
The T.H.C. made this point in its 1965 *Annual Report:*

... road transport needs a supervision that is local and immediate,
and capable of taking decisions. The services must be constantly
fitted in with the particular and fluctuating demands of customers
... what is needed is direct, fully responsible management, on the
job, and a strong but short chain of managerial command.

The survival of so many small firms in the industry might
suggest that there are no significant economies of scale in
road transport and that B.R.S. was therefore unnecessarily
large. But the market for road haulage is imperfect and localized, and those sectors of B.R.S. activities which operated
within the local markets were decentralized in management
and administration to compete with small hauliers. For other
types of activity such as general haulage there are probably
technical economies of large-scale operation, in respect of
more intensive use of vehicles and higher load factors, better
routing of services, better utilization of labour, more mechan-

ical handling in depots, and so on. Also the existence of a national network operating under one name should tend to mean a greater customer awareness and use. In these respects BRS probably gained from its size and national coverage, and there were presumably economies in setting up specialist companies to deal with particular types of traffic, within the general administrative framework of B.R.S. as a whole. The existence of economies of scale could only be proved by an examination of the unit costs of large firms such as those controlled by B.R.S. and of small operators, but no estimates of their relative costs exist. The most we can do is to indicate the structure of operating costs of B.R.S. and compare this with the rough average for the whole industry, and this is done in Table 24.

The B.R.S. data conceal considerable variations between

Table 24
Cost Structure of B.R.S. and the Industry, 1967

Working expenses	Per cent of total	
	BRS	Industry
Wages of drivers and mates	26·8	40–45
Fuel, tyres, vehicle licences	16·2	
Other operating costs	3·6	30–35
Repairs to vehicles	9·0	
Depreciation of vehicles	7·7	10
Depot expenses	13·4	
Other, including insurance and administration	23·1	10–20
Total	100	100

Sources: B.R.S.—T.H.C., *Annual Report 1967*, p. 57.
Industry—National Board for Prices and Incomes (1965), Report no. 1, *Road Haulage Rates*, H.M.S.O., Cmnd 2695; and National Board for Prices and Incomes (1967), Report no. 48, *Charges, Costs and Wages in the Road Haulage Industry*, H.M.S.O., Cmnd 3482.

groupings. In B.R.S. parcels, for example, depot staff costs accounted for 28 per cent of total costs.

The data for the industry as a whole do not adequately reflect the great differences between firms. The Prices and Incomes Board Report[1] noted that the wages of drivers and mates ranged from 25 to 50 per cent of total costs in different firms. A high proportion of costs are fixed and are independent of mileage, so that the higher the utilization of vehicles and drivers, the lower are unit costs. The table also shows that a large proportion of costs can apparently be attributed quite directly to particular vehicles and services. There are no 'track costs' in road haulage as there are in the railways, and the problem of allocating joint and overhead costs is thus much less serious. This would suggest that road hauliers should be able to relate the price of a service quite closely to the cost of providing that service, but the practice of pricing in the industry is much more complicated, so far as one can tell on the basis of the little information available.

Up to 1965 the Road Haulage Association made periodic recommendations to its members on increases in rates, based on the general trend of the cost of wages and vehicle operation. These recommendations stopped in 1965, after the Prices and Incomes Board had observed that the variation in costs and productivity throughout the industry was much too wide to warrant general over-all increases. In any case many hauliers did not follow the recommendations in their published prices, and these published prices were very often not the rates actually charged. Very many individual factors determine the rate which is actually charged for a particular consignment on a particular service. These include the operating cost of the vehicle, the characteristics of the cargo (e.g. weight, size, ease of loading, etc.), time taken, allocation of overheads, the probability of securing a return load rather than having to send back the vehicle empty, and likely competition from other hauliers for the available business. All these points make it desirable that the pricing decision

1. Prices and Incomes Board, Report no. 48, p.6.

for a particular journey or consignment should be taken as close to the customer as possible, and one reason for the Transport Holding Company's insistence on decentralized management was to allow this necessary flexibility in price-setting.

Nevertheless one might have expected that in B.R.S., as distinct from some of the smaller concerns in the industry, pricing decisions would have been related to costs as far as possible, but this was not the case in B.R.S. Parcels grouping, which was examined by the Prices and Incomes Board in 1967. Indeed the Board noted that B.R.S. Parcels did not have the cost information necessary to allow such a pricing policy.

It is not known how far the tariff structure reflects the cost structure since the company has not hitherto considered it worth while to undertake the complex studies necessary to determine the structure of costs in relation to the volume, weight and distance of parcel. While we recognise that in the short run costs are not the sole determinants of charges, in the long run there should in our view be a definite relationship between them.[1]

The formulation of rational pricing policies in B.R.S. Parcels was thought to be particularly important 'since the Company acts, in the main, as price leader and thus any distortion in its charges is likely to be reflected throughout this sector of the industry.'[2] In fact B.R.S. published prices in the general haulage sector also tended to have an effect on the prices charged by other firms, partly because the company acted as price leader but also because B.R.S. prices were commonly used as the starting point from which other hauliers and B.R.S. itself would bargain with their customers. This type of competition is another reason why B.R.S. had to adopt a flexible and decentralized pricing policy, and why prices could not in the short run be related only to costs.

Table 25 gives some indication of the profitability of the T.H.C. and its road haulage subsidiaries.

1. Prices and Incomes Board, Report no. 48, p.20.
2. ibid., p.23.

Table 25
T.H.C. and its Road Haulage Profit Rates 1963–7

	1963	1964	1965	1966	1967
1. T.H.C. profits as per cent of average capital employed	9·5	11·6	10·9	8·2	5·4
2. B.R.S. profits as per cent of average capital employed	8·3	12·5	11·1	6·8	3·8
Road haulage groupings profits as per cent of gross revenue					
3. General	3·5	7·4	6·0	2·9	1·2
4. Parcels	12·1	15·2	12·8	5·4	3·8
5. Pickfords	11·7	12·2	11·3	11·1	9·3
6. Total B.R.S.	7·5	10·5	8·8	5·5	3·3

Note: Profits are before tax. Lines 1 and 2 express profits as a percentage of capital employed (mean of beginning and end of year); lines 3–6 express profits as a percentage of gross revenue.

Source: Transport Holding Company, *Annual Reports*.

Table 25 shows that in 1964–5 the road haulage interests (B.R.S.) showed a higher rate of profit than the T.H.C. as a whole, but in 1966–7 their rate of profit fell sharply. This was partly due to the effects of the prices and incomes policy, since applications for rate increases were frozen pending the Prices and Incomes Board investigation. Line 6 shows B.R.S. profits as a percentage of gross revenue, and the fall in the profit rate was less than that in line 2. We may therefore assume that the profit rates of the various groupings in lines 3–5 would have been lower had they been calculated as a percentage of average capital employed. As it is, the profitability of the Parcels grouping was badly affected by the standstill in charges, and so to a lesser extent was the General grouping which also suffered from the effect of the economic slowdown on some of its customer industries, e.g. steel and vehicles. However, the General grouping has had a consistently lower rate of profit than the other groupings, largely because of the highly competitive and not very profitable general haulage activities. The contract division within the General grouping maintained its profit in 1967, while the Pickford's grouping of more specialized activities showed only a slight fall. There is therefore some evidence that it is more profitable to concentrate on specialist or contract-type traffic than on general activities.

In conclusion, we may make two general points about the nationalized road haulage sector in the period up to 1968. Firstly, though no clear-cut evidence of economies of scale exists, there were probably advantages to the customer in having one company of national coverage and importance to carry certain types of traffic, notably trunk haulage and parcels, where better utilization of vehicles and more efficient routing can be obtained with an extensive network of services. Secondly, the Transport Holding Company operated in such a way that nationalization made very little difference to the way B.R.S. operated. Since B.R.S. had a minority share of the market and since competition was fierce, the T.H.C. had to organize its activities so that B.R.S. could operate as an effective commercial business. As we have seen, this was done through a network of financially independent subsidiary companies. There was a decentralized management structure and very little detailed politically-motivated control, though the industry was something of a political shuttlecock in the period 1947–53. In the period of the Transport Holding Company's control from 1963–7, the nationalized road haulage sector was able to combine public ownership with commercial enterprise, such that the 1967 White Paper could conclude that 'the Transport Holding Company has been conspicuously successful in tackling the problems of handling general merchandise and parcels traffic'.[1] Nonetheless under the Transport Act 1968 the T.H.C. was dissolved, and Government policy towards freight transport moved towards a greater degree of integration and co-ordination between road and rail goods transport. The implications of the Transport

1. *The Transport of Freight*, p.5.

Act for nationalized road haulage are discussed in the next section.

3. The Transport Act 1968 and its Implications

The purposes of the Transport Act 1968 can be most easily understood in the context of the White Paper to which it gave effect.[1] This proposed several objectives, the most important being to offer a more efficient freight service in the public sector partly by eliminating wasteful and inefficient competition between nationalized road and rail carriers; to use existing assets more efficiently and in particular 'to make the maximum economic use of the railways... by promoting the transfer of all suitable traffic from congested roads on to the railways';[2] and to improve safety and efficiency in road haulage by a new system of licensing and control of drivers' hours. The achievement of these objectives meant sweeping changes in the organization of the nationalized road haulage sector and in the legal framework within which the whole industry operated.

Within the nationalized transport sector, a complete redistribution of freight activities occurred. The central body is the National Freight Corporation (N.F.C.) which took over three groups of assets. These were:

1. The Transport Holding Company's road haulage (and shipping) interests.

2. The depots, vehicles, containers, etc., used in the freight-liner services by the British Railways Board – in fact all freightliner assets except the trains.

3. The British Railways Board's sundries traffic.

The N.F.C. is a holding company and will control and organize its road haulage interests through subsidiary companies as did the Transport Holding Company up to 1968. The Transport Act 1968 also established two new statutory companies as subsidiaries of the N.F.C. One, National

1. *Transport Act*, 1968, ch. 73. References will be made to sections of the Act. The White Paper was *The Transport of Freight*.
2. *The Transport of Freight*, p.3.

Carriers Ltd, is wholly owned by the N.F.C. This company was likely to be unprofitable initially, and was given a subsidy to meet initial losses over the first five years: as chapter 5 showed, the B.R.B. sundries traffic lost £26 million in 1967. The other company is the important Freightliner Company, owned 51 per cent by the N.F.C. and 49 per cent by the British Railways Board. The Freightliner Company is to be run as a commercial concern which the British Railways Board charges commercial rates for the carriage by rail of its containers. The intention is that the Freightliner Company should allow private hauliers or other traders access to the terminals and the freightliner service. In these respects the service is to be run on a commercial basis, but the National Freight Corporation is also statutorily required

to secure that, in the provision of [properly integrated] services, goods are carried by rail whenever such carriage is efficient and economic ... [with] due regard to any indication of the needs of the person for whom the goods in question are to be carried and to the nature of the goods (sec. 1a).

The fulfilment of this obligation is reinforced by the changes in the vehicle licensing system.

Under the Transport Act all vehicles with a plated weight[1] not exceeding $3\frac{1}{2}$ tons are completely exempt from licensing no matter what kind of traffic they carry. Vehicles above this size are subject to quality licensing which is designed primarily to improve safety within a competitive framework of road haulage. Quality licences are given to carriers who are capable of keeping proper control over loading and their drivers' working hours,[2] who have financial resources to maintain

1. The plated weight is the maximum payload of the vehicle. The Road Traffic Act 1967 provided for the display of a plate indicating maximum legal payload.

2. The Transport Act 1968 reduced the maximum premissible working day from fourteen to eleven hours; placed a new limit on the working week; and revised the rest period regulations. It also provided for the installation of recording equipment (tachographs) in vehicles to check on driving time.

vehicles properly, and who hold (or employ someone who holds) a transport managers' licence. This latter licence is granted to individuals in accordance with their experience and competence. Objections to a quality licence can only be made on the basis of these criteria and not on the basis of the adequacy of the existing service as was the case before 1968. The previous distinction between hauliers and own-account carriers disappears and licensed vehicles are free to undertake any kind of work. The quality licensing system therefore attempts to promote competition and efficiency in the use of vehicles, combined with stringently applied safety regulations. For vehicles over sixteen tons plated weight, however, the Act proposed *quantity* licensing, intended to come into operation during 1970. Though the Conservative Government decided not to introduce quantity licensing, it remains interesting to consider the arguments for such a system.

The objective of quantity licensing was simply to ensure that where rail services are available they should be used, unless the consignor can show that haulage by road is as good as or better than that by rail, in terms of speed, reliability and cost. In the White Paper the Government noted that competition itself ought in theory to be able to bring about the efficient allocation of traffic between road and rail, but that in practice there was a great deal of inertia and habit in consignors' behaviour. In fact, they 'may not even be aware of the advantage to them of the new rail services, nor of the true economic cost of their present arrangements'.[1] The Transport Act therefore provided that special authorization would be needed for a vehicle over sixteen tons to carry any goods for more than 100 miles, or particular goods suitable to railway carriage for any distance. Applications for special authorization or quantity licences were to be made by the consignor to the licensing authorities, and the only bodies entitled to object to the granting of a licence were the N.F.C. and the British Railways Board. Other road hauliers had no rights of ob-

1. *The Transport of Freight*, p. 16.

jection. The only ground on which objections rested was that the service could be economically provided by freight-liner or rail. If an objection was lodged, the licensing authority must decide on the basis of evidence laid before it by both applicant and objectors whether the service by rail would be less advantageous than that which the applicant proposes to offer by road, taking into account

speed, reliability, cost and such other matters relevant to the needs of the person for whom the goods in question are to be carried as may be prescribed (sec. 74, 5).

If the service by rail was judged to be less advantageous or even if it appeared equally advantageous, the application was granted and a quantity licence given: in other words, for an objection to succeed, the N.F.C. and/or the B.R.B. had to prove that rail had a definite advantage over the applicant's proposals. These new licensing procedures and regulations would have a great effect on the road haulage industry, and on the nationalized sector operated by the National Freight Corporation.

So far as small goods vehicles are concerned, the Transport Act sets up a wholly competitive framework. No licence is required and entry to the industry is completely free, provided the operator complies with the road safety regulations. The distinction between own-account carriage and carriage for hire and reward has disappeared, and we might therefore expect greater competition in this sector. However it seems likely that most small goods vehicles are used for own-account deliveries, and the abolition of the licensing system might make relatively little difference to the structure of the industry. It is in the larger size-ranges of vehicles (above $3\frac{1}{2}$ tons plated weight) that the Transport Act will have most effect. Previously a licence to carry for hire and reward was only granted provided existing services were in some way inadequate, though C licences for own-account traffic were granted freely. Under the quality licensing system, the criteria for a licence depend on the fitness and competence of the operator and not on the actual or potential demand for his services. This again means that entry to the industry may be much easier, and competition to existing operators is likely to increase. However, this depends on the attitude of the licensing authorities. By specifying high standards of fitness and competence for operators, they could still limit entry only to very well-qualified applicants.

A major reason why one might expect competition in the industry to increase, even if there is still some restriction on entry, comes from the abolition of different licence types. Vehicle operators who normally carry own-account traffic will be free to carry for hire and reward if they wish, so entering the market previously held by the road hauliers. One of the main problems of the C licensing system was that vehicles carrying own-account traffic on a long-distance trip often had to make an empty return journey simply because the operator had no goods of his own which he wished to carry on the return journey. Under the quality licensing system, own-account trunk hauliers will be able to carry for hire and reward on return trips, so increasing their vehicle utilization and over-all efficiency. Moreover, the own-account carrier is in a very favourable position to charge a low price for this service. His main purpose was to carry goods on the outward journey, and since the vehicle must in any case get back to its base whether empty or loaded, the marginal cost of carrying goods on the return trip is very low. The main problem of the own-account haulier with an empty return trip is to find a consignor who wishes to send goods on that route and to find him quickly, since it may be more efficient for the own-account operator to return his vehicles empty rather than to search around for a return load. There is obviously scope for a growth in the service of 'loadbrokers' who would bring together hauliers with space on their vehicles and consignors with goods to send.[1] Some large own-account operators with regular services and an established network of

1. Some firms already existed before 1968 to provide this service for A licence hauliers but were not particularly important.

routes and depots might expand into commercial road haulage on a more regular basis.

All these developments would increase competition in the road haulage industry, and the entry of new firms or the expansion of existing ones would have a particular effect on those carriers previously holding A licences who were in some measure protected from new entrants and from outright C licence competition. This being so, it seems inevitable that the various companies of British Road Services, especially the general haulage companies, will face stiffer competition in the future than they did in the past. Another possible problem for B.R.S., now of course under the control of the National Freight Corporation, is the statutory duty of the N.F.C. to use railways as far as possible where this is efficient and economic. The White Paper explained:

The two undertakings [N.F.C. and B.R.B.] will be expected to invest in new freightliner services wherever the return on capital to them jointly would be better than if the investment were not made and the traffic continued to go throughout by road.[1]

The N.F.C. will therefore have to consider the joint interest of the freightliner company when deciding the mode by which goods should be sent, not to mention its own considerable investment in fixed capital in the freightliner terminals and other assets. The achievement of high volume traffic on the freightliner service may require the diversion of traffic from road to rail, even though it would have been profitable for the N.F.C. itself to have sent the goods by road.

Though quantity licensing was not introduced, the legislation represented an attempt to make consumers' transport decisions rational. What would be the effect if, at some time in the future, quantity licensing did come into effect? Special authorization would be needed for journeys of over 100 miles by vehicles of over sixteen tons plated weight, and for shorter journeys where the vehicles were carrying bulk commodities (such as coal, iron and steel, cement, etc.)

1. *The Transport of Freight*, p. 6.

which rail is well suited to carry. There are two unknown factors here. Firstly, how many consignors are sending goods of these kinds by road in ignorance of the cost and convenience of sending them by rail? Evidence does suggest that many own-account fleet owners have little idea of their present transport costs,[1] and a licensing system which forced them to consider the railways would also force them to compare real transport costs. The result might be a large switch to the railways on rational economic grounds which gave a more efficient over-all transport mode, but which meant a significant decline in the amount going by road trunk haulage. Secondly, how will the licensing authorities adjudicate in cases where objections have been raised, and what weight will they give to the various factors mentioned in the Transport Act as being relevant to the consignor's choice of mode? For example, if a consignor values the flexibility of road transport so much that he is willing to pay more for road carriage than he would by rail, will he be granted a special authorization or will the licensing authorities decide that he should send goods by rail? Clearly the licensing authorities cannot always accept the consignor's view of things, otherwise all applications for special authorizations would be granted, except where the consignor had been in ignorance of the costs and advantages of rail carriage.

It was obvious that the Transport Act 1968 would have a considerable effect on nationalized road haulage. The quality licensing system allowed for more freedom of entry into the industry by competent operators, so that private hauliers and own-account operators would be bidding for the available traffic. The statutory obligation of the N.F.C. to use rail wherever this was economic, and the desire of the N.F.C. and British Rail to profit jointly from freightliners, could have meant a diversion of traffic from road to rail. The logical course of action for the N.F.C. was to follow the policy of the Transport Holding Company, and to concentrate a greater share of its resources on operating specialised services which

1. See, for example, Ministry of Transport (1968), *Transport for Industry*, H.M.S.O.

were not direct competitors with the railways, or in which road had the comparative advantage.

In fact, by 1972 it was clear that the N.F.C. had successfully managed the transition, and despite the sluggish growth of the economy and the consequent depression of freight traffic, the N.F.C. had shown improvements in profitability and productivity. Indeed, the Corporation expected to show a small profit in 1972, in spite of the economic difficulties and the Government's price freeze, compared with a loss of £1·6 million in 1971. The success of the N.F.C. is exemplified in the experience of National Carriers Ltd., which was taken over from British Rail in 1968, and in respect of which the N.F.C. had available a subsidy of £60 million over the period 1969–73. The operating loss of N.C.L. has been sharply reduced, from £15 million in 1969 to about £4 million in 1972, and the total amount of aid received up to 1972 was £41 million. The N.F.C. hoped that National Carriers would break even in 1973 without further assistance.

In its Annual Report for 1971, the N.F.C. set out its management philosophy, that 'a company-based structure, with responsibility firmly placed on the managing director of each company and with each company clearly defined as a profit centre, best suits road transport and the business of the Corporation.' (p. 28)

The N.F.C. was organised into seven operating groups, including B.R.S., Special Traffics, and Pickfords International, each containing a number of related companies, and each with a group co-ordinator to oversee the profit, performance and health of the group. Here the N.F.C. see a difference between their organisation and that of the Transport Holding Company: 'The change from the conglomerate nature [of the T.H.C.] to an intensively freight oriented organisation … requires … rather more central coordination than that which suited the T.H.C.' (p. 28)

Thus the Board of the N.F.C. in 1971 laid down guidelines for the operating companies, paying attention to costs, cash flow, and profitability, and with the effective use of resources as the basic objective. This concentration of efficiency and flexibility should pay dividends as the economy grows more rapidly and freight transport recovers from the depressed conditions of 1971/2.

7 The Air Corporations

1. Introduction

In the nationalized air transport sector two public corporations operate, serving different geographical areas and carrying different types of traffic. British European Airways (BEA) operates short and medium-haul routes within Britain and to and from Europe and the Middle East, while the British Overseas Airways Corporation (BOAC) is responsible for long-distance international flights to North America, Africa, Asia, Australia, the Caribbean and the Pacific. The two corporations with their separate markets have somewhat different problems and are best discussed individually, but the essential facts of the economics of airline operation affect both airlines, and a certain amount of background information is relevant to both. This first section therefore outlines the trends in the demand for air travel and the important factors in the operation of companies which attempt to meet that demand. Section 2 sketches the framework of the licensing arrangements within which British air transport carriers operate, while sections 3 and 4 deal with B.E.A. and B.O.A.C. respectively.

The advantage which air transport offers over surface transport is basically speed of transit, and the longer the distance of the journey the more important does time saving become. The demand for air travel has been expanding very rapidly both for passenger traffic and for air freight, but since freight is still a minor part of total air transport this chapter will concentrate on passenger services.[1] Over the past ten years, the total number of passenger-miles has increased at an average rate of 15 per cent per annum.[2] The International Civil Aviation Organisation estimated that in 1968 passenger mileage on all scheduled services in its 116 member countries was some 13 per cent above 1967, which was in turn 19 per cent above 1966. Passenger mileage on scheduled services operated by British airlines doubled between 1960/61 and 1966/7, an average annual increase of about 15 per cent. As a result, most passenger movement into and out of the United Kingdom is by air; in 1967/8 60 per cent of those travelling to and from Europe and 85 per cent of those travelling to and from the rest of the world went by air. Inside the United Kingdom surface operators are able to compete quite effectively with air transport since the distances are relatively short, but on the internal domestic trunk routes such as London to Glasgow, Edinburgh and Belfast, air transport has been securing an increasing share of traffic carried by commercial operators.

B.E.A. and B.O.A.C. carry most of the air passenger traffic originating within the United Kingdom, and against this background of growing demand for air travel they must decide how much capacity to offer in order to carry this traffic. A major problem in this is the forecasting of demand. In the past, the rate of growth of demand has shown large fluctuations from year to year and it has also varied considerably as between particular routes. After making an estimate of total demand, each airline must attempt to predict its share of the market. This is made more difficult by the fact that B.E.A. and B.O.A.C. face competition from other airline

1. Passenger flights often carry freight and mail as well, and their contribution to revenue is in many cases important in making the service profitable.

2. International statistics of air transport come from the International Civil Aviation Organization and the International Air Transport Association; domestic statistics are published in various sources by the Board of Trade. The data presented here refer only to scheduled services, and do not include non-scheduled charter traffic which will be discussed later, nor private air transport which we do not discuss.

operators on all their routes, domestic and international. However, once they have made their demand forecasts, the airlines must decide how much capacity to provide in order to meet that demand. In the aggregate this means supplying a certain number of seat-miles, but in practice there are different ways of providing capacity and the airlines must decide what the most efficient operating policy would be. The total number of seat-miles made available depends on three things: the number of aircraft, the number of seats per aircraft, and the number of hours each aircraft flies. These three are to some extent substitutes for one another in that a given number of seat-miles can be made up of a different combination of aircraft number, aircraft size and aircraft utilization. What factors will an airline consider in arriving at the right operating pattern?

Firstly, it must have aircraft to match its route network. Particular aircraft are designed to fly economically and efficiently on stages of particular lengths, and to use an aircraft on a stage-length below its designed cruising range will raise unit costs. A medium-range aircraft (800–1700 miles) will be much less economic on a short stage of 400 miles than a short-range aircraft of equivalent size. Secondly, it will try to use the largest aircraft possible since within a given technology and aircraft type there are economies of scale in the operation of aircraft: 'if all other characteristics of design are held constant, each doubling of aircraft size will produce a 15 per cent reduction in seat-mile operating costs.'[1] Thirdly, more intensive use of aircraft reduces unit costs since fixed costs are spread over a longer operating period, though there is a level of annual utilization beyond which rapidly rising maintenance costs make further use uneconomic. Fourthly, there are certain rigidities in supply which may make it difficult to adjust capacity to short-run fluctuations in demand. An obvious example is that it normally takes one to two years for the order and delivery of aircraft (much longer

1. Select Committee on Nationalised Industries (1967), *British European Airways*, H.M.S.O., p. 306.

if it is a completely new type) and once aircraft have been brought into operation and services scheduled, it may well be against the airline's long-term commercial interest to reduce the frequency of services if demand is sluggish. So long as aircraft are covering their variable costs with some contribution to fixed costs, it is better to have them flying than standing idle.

The measure of an airline's success in matching capacity to demand is the *load factor*, which is simply the load carried as a proportion of capacity available. For passengers, the load factor is the number of passenger-miles as a proportion of the number of seat-miles offered. The higher the load factor the greater is the utilization of capacity, but this alone does not determine an airline's financial performance, since the capacity might be provided only at inordinate cost. To take account of this, we must introduce another concept, the break-even load factor. This is the load factor at which revenue and expenditure are just in balance. If the actual load factor exceeds the break-even load factor, the airline will make a profit, and vice versa. However, airlines cannot achieve a profitable position by charging whatever fares and running whatever services they wish. The domestic and international air transport industry is subject to a very high degree of regulation, and before we discuss the experience of B.E.A. and B.O.A.C. in sections 3 and 4 we must outline the system of 'regulated competition' within which they operate.

2. The Regulation of Competition

The British Government's control of the operations of B.E.A., B.O.A.C. and other British airlines up until 1971 was that specified by the Civil Aviation (licensing) Act 1960, which was administered by the Air Transport Licensing Board. The framework was changed in 1971 with the Civil Aviation Act. This set up the British Airways Board, and the Civil Aviation Authority (C.A.A.). The British Airways Board has no direct

regulatory function. Its remit is overall responsibility for
B.E.A. and B.O.A.C., whose chief executives serve on the
Board. Among its responsibilities are the appointment of
board members to the nationalized corporations, and the
continuous review of their policies, though not their day-to-
day operations.

The C.A.A. is the body which regulates British civil aviation.
It took over the functions of the A.T.L.B. and the Air Regis-
tration Board and is therefore responsible for the execution
of the Government's aviation policy. This includes the efficient
and economic operation of services, 'at the lowest charges
consistent with a high standard of safety', and the encouragement of independent airlines. More specifically, the C.A.A.
is responsible for granting licences to airlines to operate
particular services. Applications are considered in relation to
an applicant's fitness and competence to operate the proposed
service. As well as allocating licences, the C.A.A. has the
responsibility for fixing domestic airfares and hears applications for fare increases or reductions by any of the domestic
carriers.

The regulations as regards international traffic are much
more complex. As well as receiving a licence from the British
Government, a British operator must secure landing rights
for every scheduled service he wishes to operate. These international traffic rights are normally the result of bilateral
negotiations between governments and usually only one national operator is recognized on each route. Up to 1971
B.O.A.C. had sole British landing rights for scheduled services
to the United States, and B.E.A. had sole British traffic rights
on the routes it flies to most European countries, with
reciprocal rights being granted to European national carriers
in London.[1] Independent British airlines did have scheduled

---

1. In the case of long-haul services which B.O.A.C. operates, there
is a category of traffic known as 'fifth freedom' traffic. This simply
means that an airline of Country A has the right to land in Country B
and convey passengers to Country C. Fifth freedom traffic is particularly
important on the North Atlantic route where many national airlines

services to the same countries as B.E.A., but not on the same routes. They usually fly to different cities from B.E.A. and their scheduled services often originate in the provinces rather than London. The operation of other international routes by independent British airlines has therefore depended on international traffic rights as well as on the granting of licences by the C.A.A.

Another aspect of regulation is that all carriers flying scheduled services on an international route must charge the same fare. Since 1945 international fares have been fixed by periodic conferences of the International Air Transport Association (I.A.T.A.), where the world's airlines, except those of Russia and China, attempt to reach agreement on the level and structure of fares. The result is inevitably a compromise and up to 1972 there was no price competition in scheduled air fares, apart from occasional departures from the rules. This situation changed drastically in 1972 as we shall see. A further restriction of competition between airlines is the pooling arrangements negotiated between airlines on particular routes. B.E.A. has pooling arrangements with the other European national airlines on almost all its European routes, and B.O.A.C. has similar agreements with other airlines operating on its routes, though not on its United States services. Under pooling arrangements, the airlines serving a particular route decide beforehand on the amount of capacity each will offer, and agree to pool all revenue and split it between them according to the share of capacity each has provided. Under a normal competitive system, an airline's share of total revenue would of course be in proportion to passengers carried, not capacity made available as is the case under the pooling arrangements.

The agreement on capacity to be offered is usually the stumbling block to the granting of traffic rights to British independent airlines to fly B.E.A.'s or B.O.A.C.'s routes. A

stop over at London on the way to and from the United States. In 1963 fifth freedom traffic amounted to 11–12 per cent of total U.K./ U.S.A. traffic.

second British carrier would probably be allowed only on condition that it shared the British part of agreed capacity (and revenue), i.e. there would simply be diversion of traffic from one British operator to another. Pooling agreements are said to have advantages for both the airlines and their passengers. Firstly, they allow the companies to spread capacity more evenly throughout the day, rather than concentrating all flights on the periods of maximum demand, thus giving passengers a greater choice of departure times. Load factors are thereby improved and unit operating costs reduced. Secondly, the airlines can attempt together to increase the total market and maximize total revenue, instead of competing wastefully for a larger individual custom. Thirdly, there may be operating economies through the sharing of facilities. We shall return to the question of pooling arrangements in the next section, but it is important to remember that they are only one aspect of the tight framework of regulation which surrounds air transport.

A number of reasons are usually put forward to explain why airline operations must be closely regulated.[1] Some of these reasons are connected with the ostensible strategic or prestige benefits of maintaining a national airline, but the main economic reason is that free and unrestricted competition might lead to a price war with prices being reduced well below costs. Operators might then observe less strict safety standards in an attempt to reduce costs, or alternatively smaller and weaker airlines might go out of business. This would mean a decline in the quality of service to the passenger, who would be at the mercy of the service offered and price charged by the dominant supplier(s). It is the possible ill-effects of this tendency to oligopoly or monopoly that these regulations are said to check. Up to 1972, these regulations made it virtually impossible for an airline to change unilaterally the capacity offered or the price it charged, and this made efficiency of operation and reduction of unit costs most

1. See Wheatcroft, S. (1964), *Air Transport Policy*, Michael Joseph, for a discussion of these.

important. With this in mind we now examine the recent experience of B.E.A. and B.O.A.C.

3. British European Airways

Several important questions arise in a discussion of B.E.A. How well has the airline performed in terms of increasing traffic and matching capacity to the growth of demand? How effectively has it met competition from other airlines? How far have its equipment choice and economic policy enabled it to reduce costs and achieve a good financial record? Table 26 provides some traffic and operating statistics for B.E.A. for the years 1960/61 and 1967/8, and these give some indication of the airline's performance.

In spite of the fact that 1967/8 was a poor year for B.E.A.[1], the period between 1960/61 and 1967/8 saw substantial increases in capacity and in both passenger and freight traffic, particularly in freight traffic where freight ton-miles increased twice as fast as passenger-miles over the seven-year period. However, because freight is still a relatively small part of B.E.A. traffic, freight revenue in 1967/8 being less than 10 per cent of total revenue, we shall concentrate on the passenger traffic. Table 26 shows that passenger-miles rose more rapidly than total passengers carried, reflecting the increase in average journey length. Also, though the number of aircraft hardly increased at all (the 1967/8 aircraft were on average half as big again as those in 1960/61), they showed a faster block speed, and they were used more intensively with the average number of revenue hours rising from 1990 hours to 2254 hours. As a consequence of the larger and faster aircraft and their more intensive use, capacity ton-miles per aircraft and total capacity offered expanded by 140 per cent. But demand, as measured by both load ton-miles and passenger-miles, grew more slowly than capacity so that both the over-all

1. 1967/8 held many problems for B.E.A. Traffic rose very little, the restricted foreign travel allowance hit holiday traffic, the Middle East war affected operations, and devaluation increased costs. Had 1967/8 been 'normal' some of the performance improvements in Table 26 would have been greater.

Table 26

B.E.A. Traffic and Operating Statistics, 1960/61 and 1967/8

	1960/61	1967/8	Per cent increase
Traffic			
Capacity ton-miles (millions)*	237·4	569·6	+140
Load ton-miles (millions)*	154·7	330·7	+114
Over-all load factor	65·2%	58·1%	—
Passengers (millions)	4·0	7·3	+84
Passenger-miles (millions)	1393	2728	+96
Passenger load factor	66·7%	60·2%	—
Freight ton-miles (000)	16,601	46,063	+177
Aircraft			
Effective number of aircraft	93	96	+ 4
Seats available per flight	56	86	+ 54
Revenue hours per aircraft	1990	2254	+ 13
Capacity ton-miles per aircraft (000)	2442	5851	+140
Operations			
Route mileage	47,016	59,357	+ 26
Stage distance (miles)	288	344	+ 19
Average block speed (m.p.h.)**	205	264	+ 29

Notes: *Capacity ton-miles is the payload of the aircraft multiplied by the distance flown, load ton-miles is the load carried multiplied by distance flown.

**Average block speed is the average speed over the whole stage length, including climb to and descent from cruising height.

Source: British European Airways, *Annual Reports*.

load factor and passenger load factor fell.[1] The break-even load factor also fell, from 62·2 per cent in 1960/61 to 59·2 per cent in 1967/8, but in 1967/8 the actual load factor was below the break-even load factor so that the airline made a loss.

The falling passenger load factor illustrates from the point of view of B.E.A. how difficult it can be to tailor capacity to

1. A drop of one percentage point in passenger load factor implies a fall in annual revenue of about £1½ million.

demand. One important reason for this has been the variability of traffic. The number of passenger-miles flown by B.E.A. has never declined from one year to the next, but the rate of increase has varied between 16 per cent in 1963/4 and 1 per cent in 1967/8. A year in which traffic grows by much less than expected creates problems because it is very difficult in the short run for an airline to reduce substantially capacity or seat-miles on offer. Under the international pooling agreements capacity to be offered is agreed beforehand, and it would be a very short-sighted policy both politically and commercially for an airline to withdraw or curtail services. In any case, the cost structure of airline operations suggests that this would be of limited effectiveness: 'only about one-third of total costs can be regarded as directly variable with a short-term reduction in the amount of flying'.[1] Table 27 shows the breakdown of B.E.A.'s expenditure in 1967/8.

Table 27
Expenditure by B.E.A. 1967/8 as Per Cent of Total

Aircraft standing charges	9·5
Maintenance and overhaul	16·3
Flying operations	22·9
Passenger and cargo services	7·1
Area and station costs	21·3
Sales and publicity	10·5
Other, incl. H.Q. administration	12·4
Total	100·0

Source: British European Airways, *Annual Reports*.

It is worth noting here that an airline operating on short stage-lengths like B.E.A. will find it difficult to utilize aircraft as intensively as one with long stage-lengths, since the aircraft will spend more time on the ground turning round between flights and will have a slower average block speed. Thus aircraft standing charges have to be spread over fewer aircraft hours, and landing fees are a more important component of total costs.

1. B.E.A., *Annual Report 1958/9*, p.11.

The characteristics of airline operation and the high incidence of fixed costs explain why B.E.A. found it hard to cope with a fall in the level of traffic relative to its forecasts. Given the difficulty of altering capacity, it is not surprising that its passenger load factor fell by 2·4 percentage points in 1967/8. However, B.E.A.'s load factors have shown a downward trend over a longer period – in 1959/60 they were 9 points higher than 1967/8 – and part of the explanation for this trend is competition from other airline operators.

On domestic routes, B.E.A. had a monopoly of the important scheduled routes (i.e. London–Scotland, London–Belfast, London–Manchester, Midlands–Scotland) until 1963, when licences were granted to independent airlines to fly the important domestic trunk routes. British United Airways and British Eagle Airlines (until 1968 when it went out of business) took much of the traffic growth, especially after 1966/7 when the A.T.L.B. licensed them to increase their frequencies. As a result B.E.A.'s total passenger mileage on the London–Scotland route was virtually unchanged between 1965/6 and 1967/8, while the independents had over 12 per cent of the prime domestic air routes in 1967/8. The most effective competition came when the independents introduced jet aircraft which were both faster than B.E.A.'s turbo-prop Vanguard aircraft and also proved to have considerably more passenger appeal. To attract traffic back, B.E.A. was forced to use its own jet aircraft on a number of domestic flights. Unfortunately, the only jets B.E.A. had – Tridents and Comets – were designed for stage lengths of over 800 miles and were ill-suited to the 350 mile stage-lengths of the domestic trunk services.[1] They had higher seat-mile costs than the Vanguard aircraft which normally operated, and though B.E.A.'s jets presumably showed an over-all benefit over continued operation of Vanguards in competition with the independents' jets, B.E.A. would

1. 'A 600 m.p.h. Trident achieves a block speed of about 500 m.p.h. on a 1000 miles stage-length but only 330 m.p.h. on a stage-length of 250 miles ... this reduction in average speed on short routes has a marked effect on the unit cost level.' *British European Airways*, p.307. For stage-length cost curves, see B.E.A., *Annual Report 1968/9*, Graph 1.

obviously have greatly preferred to have no jet aircraft on offer at all rather than to have to use unprofitable jets on some flights.

Further competition on domestic routes came from British Railways' success in winning traffic to the electrified London–Manchester service, and B.E.A. London–Manchester traffic fell by 25 per cent in 1966/7, the first year of the electrified service. As a result of air and rail competition, B.E.A.'s domestic passenger load factor fell from 69 per cent in 1965/6 to 62 per cent in 1967/8, and since no pooling agreements operate on domestic flights, this competition had a considerable effect on B.E.A.'s finances.

For international traffic, competition exists on both scheduled and non-scheduled services. The competition for scheduled traffic is restricted by the standard fares charged by all airlines, by pooling arrangements, and by the bilateral negotiation of traffic rights. Non-scheduled services operate outside pooling agreements and there is no British Government restriction on the growth of this traffic, though landing rights are still necessary and there is some price restriction on inclusive tour charter holidays by air in that the total cost of the holiday, including accommodation, cannot be less than the return air fare by scheduled service. As a result of this greater freedom, non-scheduled charter services had 30 per cent of U.K.–Europe air traffic in 1967/8 compared with 15 per cent in 1962/3. Their average annual rate of growth was 22 per cent compared with only 9 per cent for scheduled traffic. These charter services were mainly for inclusive tour holidays, and tended to be seasonal: in the summer of 1967 charter traffic was 36 per cent of total U.K.–Europe traffic. The over-all effect of charter services on B.E.A. is difficult to estimate but for certain types of service it has been considerable. B.E.A. warned in 1967/8 that

B.E.A.'s share of this market has now fallen to the extent that if this policy (of unrestricted licensing) is carried to the extreme, B.E.A. may be forced to withdraw scheduled services to some continental resorts.[1]

1. B.E.A., *Annual Report 1967/8*, pp.32–3.

B.E.A. itself ran inclusive tour charters, but both these operations and those of other carriers were badly affected by the restrictions on foreign travel allowances which were imposed temporarily in 1967/8.

On scheduled services, the pooling arrangements which are negotiated route by route by the airlines concerned might appear to eliminate competition entirely, since they settle how much capacity is to be provided by each and agree that total revenue should be split between the airlines on the basis of how much capacity they have provided, rather than how many passengers they have carried. The airlines' reply is that pooling has advantages for the passenger and that in any case the system does not allow any individual airline to become less competitive than its pool partner. Pooling arrangements are agreed frequently, often twice yearly, and the airlines then examine traffic data to see whether he pool is unduly favouring one party or the other. If an airline consistently carries a smaller proportion of the total passengers than the proportion of capacity which it provides (i.e. if its load factors are consistently lower than its partner's), then the pooling agreement is unduly favouring it. This is because the revenue it pays into the pool depends on the number of passengers carried, while the amount it draws out is determined by its share of capacity made available. There is then a clear case for reapportioning the pool, either by cutting down the amount of capacity the less competitive airline is permitted to provide, or by its making extra payments to its pool partner.

The possibility of reapportionment means that each carrier must attempt at least to maintain its market share, but in practice it appears that the reapportionment of a pool only occurs where a fundamental disequilibrium in traffic shares has occurred. In evidence to the Select Committee, B.E.A.'s Chairman commented that 'a pool is a long term affair and one does not vary it merely because for a season or two seasons one side has got to better advantage through aircraft or for any other reason.'[1] Up to 1967, there was only one route where B.E.A.'s pooling arrangements were changed. This was

1. *British European Airways*, p. 213.

London–Paris, where in the early 1960s Air France, B.E.A.'s pool partners, introduced jet aircraft which attracted custom away from B.E.A.'s Vanguards, and this eventually forced a reapportionment of the pool to B.E.A.'s disadvantage. B.E.A. then introduced Trident jets which allowed it to recover some of the ground it had lost. However, this had its costs. As on the domestic trunk routes, the London–Paris stage-length was much shorter than the Trident's optimum range, and the Tridents had higher seat-mile costs than the Vanguards they replaced. The irony of the situation is that according to evidence given to the Select Committee, neither B.E.A. nor Air France made a profit on the route despite its heavy traffic, at least partly because both airlines were using unsuitable aircraft as a form of quality competition.[1]

International air transport is largely built around pooling agreements, and it is highly unlikely that they would ever be abandoned, but this system of regulation does give rise to some problems for the individual airlines. For example, B.E.A. cannot raise fares when it wishes, it cannot schedule more flights without its pool partner's agreement, and even an increase in its share of the market may not be accompanied by a corresponding increase in revenue drawn out of a pool. Given the limited courses of action open to it, the financial success of B.E.A. depends on two things. Firstly, it must attract as much custom as possible to keep load factors high and to maintain its share of pooled revenue; and secondly, it must attempt to improve aircraft utilization and reduce unit costs. In this second respect, it is most important to have efficient and competitive aircraft, for the lower the seat-mile cost of the aircraft fleet, the lower is the break-even load factor, and the better able will the airline be to withstand a fall in traffic. Unfortunately, B.E.A. has from time to time had less competitive aircraft than those of other airlines. Thus for example in the early 1960s when other international airlines were intro-

1. This indicates a basic defect of the system under which only two airlines fly a route under a pooling arrangement. If *both* airlines are inefficient or unconcerned about rising costs, they may be able to push fares up, to the detriment of the passengers.

ducing jets on their London routes, B.E.A. was caught with a shortage of jet capacity. It introduced more Comet jets while waiting for the Trident which came into full service in 1964/5, but the Trident had more than the usual introductory teething troubles, and the early Tridents did not have as good performance and operating economics as B.E.A. had expected.[1] The Tridents had high seat-mile costs and contributed relatively little to profits in their first two years, in part because they were used on unsuitable routes such as London–Glasgow and London–Paris on which they needed very high load factors to break even. The Vanguard had low seat-mile costs but had far less passenger appeal than jets, and B.E.A. acknowledged the lack of a competitive short-range aircraft in 1966 when it was forced to take a major re-equipment decision on a fleet of short-range jets and also on a fleet of new large medium-range jets to supplement the Tridents.

B.E.A.'s first choice was American Boeing aircraft, but Government permission was refused on the grounds that B.E.A. must buy British aircraft. While B.E.A. quickly decided to buy short-range B A C Super 1–11 jets, the arguments over the medium-range aircraft continued for eighteen months. During 1967 B.E.A. asked permission to order the B A C 2–11, a 200-seat aircraft then at the design stage, for which the Government was to be asked to pay all the development costs, estimated at £100 million or more. This too was refused, and in 1968 B.E.A. ordered the Trident 3B, 'an excellent aircraft from the passenger's point of view but basically too small for B.E.A.'s needs'.[2] In 1967 when the Trident 3B was at the design stage its seat-mile costs were estimated to be 9 per cent higher than those of the existing Boeing 727 which B.E.A. originally wanted.[3] The devaluation of November 1967 increased the capital cost of the Boeings and might have raised their seat-mile costs above the forecasts for the Trident 3B, but if this is not the right aircraft for B.E.A., the airline's operations are bound to be adversely affected.

1. *British European Airways*, p.109.
2. B.E.A., *Annual Report 1967/8*, p.19.
3. *British European Airways*, p.240.

In the period up to 1967/8 B.E.A.'s economic performance was quite meritorious, as Table 28 shows. In the period 1960/61 to 1967/8, B.E.A. managed to reduce cost per capacity ton-mile, and the reduction would certainly have been greater but for the bad year 1967/8 and the increased use of aircraft on unsuitable routes. Capacity ton-miles per employee rose by some 50 per cent in the same period. B.E.A.'s profit record was variable. In 1961/2 and 1967/8 the airline was badly hit by excess capacity and a fall in load factor when demand increased much more slowly than had been estimated. In 1962/3 there were very heavy aircraft introductory costs, such as the training of crews, excess engineering and maintenance costs, and an allowance for under-utilization of new aircraft. In spite of these problems, B.E.A. almost met its target rate of return of 6 per cent over the period 1962/3 to 1967/8, the average rate of return per annum being 5·7 per cent. It is, however, interesting to note that in evidence to the Select Committee B.E.A.'s Chairman expressed himself doubtful of the value of the financial incentive. B.E.A. apparently tried to produce the maximum profit each year, and raising or lowering the financial objective would have little effect on their operations. The Select Committee were understandably critical of B.E.A.'s views on the value of financial objectives.[1]

The profit data in Table 28 do not show the profitability of different services. In fact B.E.A. usually makes profits on international services, but the domestic services are chronically unprofitable, losing money every year up to 1968. For example, in 1965/6 B.E.A. made a profit of £2·98 million on international services, and a loss of £1·59 million on domestic services. Every domestic service showed a loss: for the London to Glasgow, Edinburgh and Belfast routes the deficit was 4·7 per cent of revenue on these services, for London–Manchester it was 21 per cent, and for the Scottish Highlands and Islands service it was almost 25 per cent of revenue.[2] The Highlands and Islands service has been a

1. *British European Airways*, pp. xxxii–xxxiii.
2. In 1968/9 B.E.A. lost £566,000 on the London–Glasgow route, one of the busiest routes in Europe, and £197,000 on the London–Edinburgh route.

Table 28
B.E.A.'s Productivity and Financial Performance, 1960/61 to 1967/68

| | | | | | Year ended 31 March | | | |
	1961	1962	1963	1964	1965	1966	1967	1968
Cost per capacity ton-mile (d.)	41·4	41·0	37·7	36·0	35·6	37·5	37·6	39·6
Capacity ton-miles per employee	17,930	19,460	20,288	22,701	24,701	25,592	27,073	26,599
£ million								
Total revenue	42·3	46·4	51·2	60·0	65·9	76·3	86·4	92·3
Gross profit	2·8	0·9	2·8	5·9	5·6	5·1	4·8	3·1
Net interest payable	1·3	2·3	3·1	2·8	3·2	3·8	4·1	4·9
Net profit	1·5	−1·5	−0·3	3·0	1·3	1·3	0·7	−1·8
Gross profit as % of capital employed	8·0	1·6	4·7	8·9	6·4	(6+)	5·5	(3)

Note: The figures in brackets are estimates since B.E.A. *Annual Reports* do not always give exact figures for the rate of return on capital employed. The data have been taken from the *Annual Reports*, and because of slight differences in interpretation they are consistently higher than figures published elsewhere by the Treasury.

Source: B.E.A., *Annual Reports*.

constant problem since it has always made heavy losses. B.E.A. accepts voluntarily the running of the service, but pointed out in evidence to the Select Committee that though it was impossible to see the service ever breaking even, the annual loss might be contained at about £300,000. In fact the 1967/8 loss was a record £374,000.

The question is, if these services are to be operated how should the losses be covered? One way would be by a subsidy to B.E.A., either from the Government or from the Highlands and Islands Development Board. Another would be by a capital reconstruction under which B.E.A.'s assets would be written down to reflect the fact that some of them were engaged in permanently unprofitable activities. B.E.A. favours the second solution and are opposed to a subsidy (though not necessarily to 'over-all financial support') on the grounds that it would give little incentive to reduce costs. On the other hand, a capital reconstruction would be much less precise in isolating and dealing with the loss, and there is much to be said for the Select Committee's view that a subsidy from the Highlands and Islands Development Board would be the best solution. However, it is worth noting that the losses on the recognized social service routes were taken into account by the Government when they fixed B.E.A.'s target rate of return at 6 per cent. Had B.E.A. not intended to continue these services, the target rate would have been 6½ per cent, i.e. B.E.A. would have been expected to earn a gross profit some £500,000 higher in 1967/8 than it actually did.

B.E.A.'s *Annual Report* for 1967/8 forecast problems ahead for the airline and it is easy to see why. In the period up to 1972 B.E.A. was in the throes of re-equipment. Initially it did not have the Trident 3B with which to counter the larger jets of its competitors on international services. As the aircraft came into service it was faced with substantial introductory costs of the Trident 3B and BAC 1–11.[1] To assist B.E.A. over this period the Government decided to transfer £25 million of

_____

1. B.E.A. has the practice of capitalizing introductory costs and writing them off over five years. This avoids a very heavy incidence of training and engineering costs in the first two years of an aircraft's life.

B.E.A.'s liabilities into a special non-interest-bearing account, 'from which predetermined amounts will be included in B.E.A.'s profit and loss account.'[1] Later, consideration would be given to treating a further £12 million in this way. It was stressed that this was not a subsidy; it was intended

to compensate B.E.A. generally because as a result of Government decisions it could not have the aircraft of the size it wanted at the time it wanted because we said it was not to buy American.[2]

B.E.A. benefits in two ways. Firstly, the reduction of £25 million in capital liabilities will reduce interest payable on capital, and secondly the £25 million goes directly into the revenue account. The total benefit to B.E.A.'s revenue account was about £30 million in the four years up to 1972, by which time B.E.A. had twenty-six Trident 3Bs which, it had said, were 'basically too small' for the airline's needs.

This discussion of procurement policy brings home the fact that B.E.A. is subject to a very high degree of Government control. Domestic competition and fares are regulated by the C.A.A. in accordance with Government guidelines; bilateral agreements between governments determine landing rights on international scheduled services, for which fares are also regulated; and the extent to which British airlines can compete with B.E.A. is determined by the Government. But it is in the field of procurement policy that Government control has its most important commercial effect. The decision to use British or foreign aircraft is taken by B.E.A. but has to be endorsed by the Government, in the light of the implications for the balance of payments, national prestige, and the British aircraft industry, as well as for the commercial operations of B.E.A. The principle has now been established whereby B.E.A. is compensated if the Government insists on its buying an aircraft which would not have been chosen on purely commercial grounds.

1. *Hansard*, vol. 768, 10 July 1968, cols. 522–6.
2. ibid., col. 526.

4. British Overseas Airways Corporation

In a discussion of B.O.A.C. the same questions arise as in our discussion of B.E.A. What have been the main economic trends in the operation of the airline in the past few years, what is its present position, and what appear to be the significant problems which it faces in the future? Table 29 presents B.O.A.C. traffic and operating statistics for the years 1960/61 and 1967/8.

Table 29
B.O.A.C. Traffic and Operating Statistics 1960/61 and 1967/8

	1960/61	1967/8	Per cent increase
Traffic*			
Capacity ton-miles (millions)	577·4	1456·2	+152
Load ton-miles (millions)	321·7	757·3	+135
Over-all load factor	55·7%	52·0%	
Passengers carried (thousands)	794·5	1548·3	+ 95
Passenger-miles (millions)	2445	5278·1	+116
Passenger load factor	59·8%	57·4%	
Freight ton-miles (millions)	43·7	197·5	+352
Aircraft			
Number of operational aircraft (year end)	74	46	− 38
Seats available per scheduled flight	Not available	126	—
Revenue hours per aircraft	2758	3820	+ 39
Capacity ton-miles per aircraft hour (scheduled)	3612	9043	+150
Operations			
Route mileage	Not available	249,218	—
Average stage distance (miles)	Not available	1677	—
Average block speed (m.p.h.)	347	453	+ 31

*Note: Traffic statistics refer only to scheduled services. B.O.A.C. carried 13,602 passengers on non-scheduled services in 1967–8, less than 1 per cent of total passengers carried.

Source: B.O.A.C., *Annual Reports*.

A comparison of the 1967/8 data for B.O.A.C. and B.E.A. (in Table 26) shows the different scale of operations involved in a long-range airline such as B.O.A.C. It carried only about one-fifth as many passengers as B.E.A. but flew more passenger-miles. B.O.A.C. aircraft were bigger (126 seats available against 86), B.O.A.C. stage distances were far longer (1677 miles as against 344), and its average block speeds were much higher (453 m.p.h. as against 264 m.p.h.). One consequence of the longer stage-length is that a smaller part of an aircraft's operating life is spent on the ground turning round between flights, and this is reflected in the fact that B.O.A.C. achieved an average aircraft utilization of 3820 revenue hours as against 2254 for B.E.A.

B.O.A.C.'s traffic experience over the seven-year period, 1960–67 is not dissimilar to that of B.E.A. Capacity ton-miles rose by about 150 per cent, load ton-miles by slightly less. The number of passengers carried almost doubled and the number of passenger-miles more than doubled, reflecting an increase in the average journey length. B.O.A.C.'s load factors showed the same downward trend as B.E.A.'s, the over-all load factor falling from 55·7 per cent in 1960/61 to 52 per cent in 1967/8. But there are two important differences in the case of B.O.A.C. Firstly, the number of aircraft fell sharply from seventy-four to forty-six and their average size increased; and secondly, B.O.A.C.'s break-even load factor fell by even more than its actual load factor from 52·5 per cent in 1960/61 to 43·8 per cent in 1967/8. These two features are closely related. In 1960/61 most of B.O.A.C.'s fleet were Comet jet and Britannia prop-jet aircraft, and the airline had only just taken delivery of fifteen Boeing 707s. The Comets and Britannias had far higher seat-mile costs than the larger Boeings. By 1967/8 B.O.A.C.'s fleet consisted of twenty Boeing 707s and twenty-nine V C10s. These larger faster aircraft were capable of more intensive use and required less maintenance than the B.O.A.C. fleet of 1960/61 and, partly as a result of this, operating costs per capacity ton-mile fell by about one-third between 1960/61 and 1967/68 as Table 30 shows.

Table 30
Operating Costs 1960/61 and 1967/8: Pence Per Capacity Ton-Mile

	1960/61	1967/8
Aircraft standing charges	4·81	2·37
Maintenance	7·07	3·42
Flying operations	7·19	5·06
Training and pre-operational costs	0·47	0·43
Passenger service	2·40	2·16
Station and traffic costs	2·12	1·77
Sales, administration, etc.	6·60	5·55
Deduct incidental revenue	−0·33	−0·30
	30·33	20·46

Source: B.O.A.C., *Annual Reports*.

A reduction in costs of this order, a fall in break-even load factor, and the relatively small fall in passenger load factor might suggest that B.O.A.C. had been successful in forecasting the demand for air traffic, in tailoring the supply of capacity to that demand, and in choosing a competitive aircraft fleet. However, this is only partly true. During the period 1960/61 to 1967/8 B.O.A.C. experienced a disastrous fall in traffic and in load factors, suffered a major crisis on its aircraft choice, underwent a capital reconstruction, and towards the end of the period was finally pulled round into a profitable organization.

The blackest period for B.O.A.C. was in 1961/2 and 1962/3. In 1961/2, when B.O.A.C. planned to increase capacity by one-third, passenger traffic rose by very much less than had been forecast, and in that one year, B.O.A.C.'s passenger load factor declined by ten points, from 59·8 per cent to 49·6 per cent. In 1962/3 the load factor fell by a further two points. There is evidence that B.O.A.C. was harder hit by the 1961/2 traffic recession than were other long-haul carriers, though their load factors also fell.[1] The Ministry of Aviation, in evidence to the

1. Select Committee on Nationalised Industries (1964), *British Overseas Airways Corporation*, H.M.S.O., vol. 1, p.28.

Select Committee in 1964, claimed that B.O.A.C. had a 'constant tendency to over optimism in estimates of traffic and revenue' and was reluctant to consider 'drastic measures'. Drastic measures in the form of a short-term reduction of capacity were, however, difficult because of pooling arrangements on most routes (though not on the U.S. services) and because of possible long-term commercial damage. The traffic recession of 1961/2 and the fall in load factor caused B.O.A.C. to lose over £50 million in that year alone.

The fall in load factor hit B.O.A.C. particularly hard because in 1961, when other airlines were bringing new jets into service, its aircraft fleet still consisted largely of Comet and Britannia aircraft which had high operating costs. In fact B.O.A.C. had since 1955 been facing a series of problems in deciding which long-range aircraft it should buy to replace the Comets and Britannias. The story is long and complicated and can only be outlined here,[1] but is is essential to an understanding of B.O.A.C.'s problems in the early 1960s. In 1956, the Government authorized B.O.A.C. to order fifteen Boeing 707s from the United States, and the airline also began discussing the specification of a new British aircraft, the VC10, more suitable for the Eastern and African routes than was the Boeing 707 at that time. In January 1958 an order was placed for thirty-five VC10s, for delivery in 1964/5, despite some doubts as to the performance guarantees (notably by B.O.A.C.'s own Engineering Department) and despite improvements in the Boeing 707. In 1960 it became clear that the cost of building the VC10 had been considerably underestimated, and continued production was in jeopardy. B.O.A.C. then agreed to order ten additional aircraft, and altered the over-all order to fifteen (later reduced to twelve) standard VC10s and thirty Super VC10s, the latter being an improved larger version. Thus in 1964 when the Select Committee reported, B.O.A.C. had on order forty-two VC10s whose estimated operating costs were considerably higher than those of the Boeing 707. The actual break-even load factor of the 707 was 43 per cent, compared with an estimated 49–55 per cent for

1. ibid. pp. 15–24.

the Super/Standard VC10.[1] In addition VC10 spares cost more, and introductory costs were bound to be higher than if B.O.A.C. had simply added Boeings to those already in service.

Following the receipt of the Corbett Report on B.O.A.C.'s financial situation – a report which was confidential to the Minister of Aviation – the Government issued a White Paper in November 1963. This clarified the situation considerably, for it requested from B.O.A.C. a plan for making the airline financially sound on the basis that

the Corporation must operate as a commercial concern. If the national interest ... requires some departure from commercial practice, this should only be done with the agreement or at the instance of the Minister of Aviation.[2]

A directive to B.O.A.C.'s Chairman repeated this and made the additional point that 'the choice of aircraft is a matter for the Corporation's judgment'.[3] After reviewing commercial policy and prospects, B.O.A.C. put forward in mid-1964 a plan for reconstruction which proposed to cancel all thirty Super VC10s, most of which were surplus to requirements, and to order eight Boeing 707s instead. This was unacceptable to the Government which directed B.O.A.C. to accept seventeen Super VC10s. To offset the higher costs of these aircraft and enable the airline to remain competitive, a financial reconstruction was made under the Air Corporations Act 1966. This wrote off £110 million of B.O.A.C.'s accrued liabilities including accumulated losses. Of the remaining capital liabilities of £66 million, £31 million was treated as loan capital with interest at 4 per cent, while £35 million was Exchequer (now Public) Dividend Capital on which a dividend could be declared out of profits.

1. *British Overseas Airways Corporation*, p. 23.
2. Ministry of Aviation (1963), *The Financial Problems of the British Overseas Airways Corporation*, H.M.S.O., p. 14.
3. B.O.A.C., *Annual Report 1962/3*, p. 54.

Table 31
B.O.A.C.'s Productivity and Financial Performance 1960/61 to 1967/8

| | Year ended 31 March | | | | | | | |
	1961	1962	1963	1964	1965	1966	1967	1968
Operating cost per capacity ton-mile (d.)	30·3	28·0	26·0	22·9	20·8	20·6	20·2	20·5
Capacity ton-miles per employee (000)	33·5	41·1	42·2	48·8	57·3	63·0	70·3	75·9
£ million								
Total revenue	88·0	92·7	92·4	103·8	114·4	124·7	137·4	150·3
Operating surplus	4·3	−10·5	−5·6	8·6	16·8	20·7	23·3	19·9
Group profit attributable to B.O.A.C. after interest and tax	−1·9	−50·1	−12·9	−10·4	8·9	8·1	23·9	22·5
Dividend on public dividend capital						3·5	5·3	10·0

Source: B.O.A.C., *Annual Reports.*

Table 31 gives an indication of B.O.A.C.'s financial performances over the period 1960/61 to 1967/8.

The Table shows clearly the swing between the bad years of 1961–1963, when a loss was made on operating account, and 1968 when the airline made a considerable surplus and showed a rate of return on net assets of 14·8 per cent. By 1967/8, B.O.A.C. had been put on a profitable and competitive footing. The airline had standardized its fleet of VC10s and Boeing 707s, and reaped operating and maintenance economies as a result. Indeed in 1967/8 the operating cost per capacity ton-mile of B.O.A.C. Super VC10s was very little above the 707s, 10·99d. (4·58p) against 10·13d. (4·22p). It is possible that a higher VC10 seat-mile was offset by its ability to achieve higher load factors. Certainly the VC10 (which no other large airline flies) has proved to have considerable passenger appeal because of its silence, its lower landing speed relative to the Boeing 707, and probably also because of B.O.A.C.'s adroit advertising which concentrated on differentiating the VC10 from all other aircraft. Relative to its international competitors B.O.A.C. had by the mid-1960s become one of the most successful long-haul carriers. A comparison with twelve other airlines in 1965 showed that B.O.A.C. ranked second in terms of break-even load factor, third in terms of unit cost of production, third in terms of unit maintenance costs, and fifth in terms of output (in capacity ton-miles) per employee.[1] However, a look ahead to the 1970s suggests that B.O.A.C. will face some difficult problems arising from the same causes as do B.E.A.'s problems, namely competition from other operators and the choice of equipment.

To some extent B.O.A.C. has to live in a more competitive environment than B.E.A., because fewer of its routes are run on a pooled basis with other airlines. Pooling agreements do exist on African services and those to Australia, Canada and the Far East, but not on the very important services to the United States, the Caribbean and the Pacific. On these

1. B.O.A.C., *Annual Report 1965/6*. A high ranking is favourable in all cases.

routes the airline's revenue depends directly on the share of traffic it can attract, and its profits depend on the cost of providing capacity. In its most recent equipment choice B.O.A.C. was not faced with the 'buy British' dilemma which confronted it over the VC10 and which B.E.A. met in 1966, since there was no British equivalent to the Boeing 747 'jumbo jet' which B.O.A.C. has used on its North Atlantic routes from 1971 onwards. These aircraft have a capacity of between 350 and 500 passengers depending on seating configuration, at least twice as many as the 707 or VC10. Most North Atlantic operators have ordered Boeing 747s, and many operators have other long-haul aircraft on order as well. The problem is whether the growth of over-all capacity will outstrip the rate of growth of demand, and reduce load factors below break-even point.[1]

The situation is very much akin to that at the beginning of the 1960s, when the introduction of the Boeing 707 led to a very large increase in capacity at a time when the growth of demand had temporarily slackened. Load factors fell substantially and many long-haul airlines lost money despite the fact that the 707 had a very much lower break-even load factor than older aircraft. Similarly the Boeing 747 is bound to have considerably lower seat-mile costs than 'smaller' jets such as the 707 or VC10, so that it can operate profitably at load factors below 40 per cent. The effect of the large prospective increase in capacity on airlines' *over-all* load factor could be financially catastrophic in the short term, but since aviation is a competitive industry no long-haul airline flying suitable routes can afford not to operate 747s or equivalent aircraft. For one thing, they are more efficient than current models in terms of seat-mile costs, and equally important, they are wide-fuselage aircraft with cabins about twice the diameter of present jets. The increased cabin space and the additional facilities which can be provided may well give

1. One estimate is that by mid-1968 world airlines had placed orders for 1242 jet aircraft of more than 100 seats, 400 of them long-range. This would double world capacity by 1972 (the *Economist*, 10 August 1968).

these larger jets considerable passenger appeal, and attract traffic away from smaller aircraft. Thus each airline has to order the larger aircraft to remain competitive, and each undoubtedly hopes to increase or at least maintain its share of the market.[1]

Between 1967/8 and 1972/4, B.O.A.C. plans to double capacity, partly by increasing service frequencies and extending routes, but also by introducing twelve Boeing 747s, which means a sharp increase in fixed investment. In 1966/7 and 1967/8 capital expenditure was between £20 million and £25 million per annum. In the five-year period up to 1972/3, total capital expenditure is estimated to be £401 million. Of this, £167 million is dollar expenditure largely to meet the cost of the 747s, estimated at about 300 million dollars. Though B.O.A.C. in 1967/8 earned about 23 per cent of its total revenue in the dollar area, it is not allowed to use dollar earnings to buy foreign aircraft, since its commitments 'are on so large a scale that finance with official exchange would impose an unacceptable burden on the United Kingdom balance of payments in the present situation' (*Annual Report*, 1967/8, p. 10). This means that B.O.A.C. must finance its £167 million dollar expenditure by raising capital abroad. The airline expects to cover the remaining non-dollar investment expenditure of £233 million out of profits plus obsolescence and depreciation reserves. The two major problems for B.O.A.C. in the period up to 1973 are therefore the satisfactory financing of the new large aircraft, and the achievement of sufficiently high load factors to maintain the airline's recent favourable profit record.

5. Conclusion

By the end of 1972, a number of important developments had

1. Similar reasoning explains why most long-haul airlines have options to buy supersonic airliners though they would undoubtedly like to postpone the very heavy capital expenditure until the end of the 1970s. If one airline decides to order such aircraft, the others must do so too, as a defensive measure.

occurred in both the organization of civil aviation services and the conditions under which the airlines operated. First the Edwards Committee, which reported in May 1969, had recommended the creation of a 'second force' airline to compete with the nationalized corporations. This private sector airline was British Caledonian, a merger of British United Airways and Caledonian Airways, one of the most successful charter operators of the 1960s. British Caledonian already ran scheduled services, including those to South America and some European cities, and in 1971 it was given routes worth about £6 million in revenue which had previously been served by B.O.A. and B.O.A.C. These included B.O.A.C.'s West African routes and a London–Paris service: in spring of 1973, British Caledonian are due to begin air services to New York and Los Angeles in competition with B.O.A.C.

Not unnaturally, both nationalized airlines were upset by the decision on the second force airline, especially as it came at a time when world airline capacity was outrunning world demand. The introduction of the Boeing 747s and other wide-bodied jets had provided an enormous increase in the number of seats available, at a time when there was a drop in the rate of increase in demand. This meant that all airlines suffered financially especially those flying very competitive routes such as the North Atlantic. In 1971/72 B.O.A.C. made an operating surplus of only £2 million about one-third of the previous year. Other airlines were much worse off. Pan American Airways, which had by far the biggest jumbo jet fleet, made its first loss ever in 1969, of £10½ million, and since then has plunged deeper into the red. Other Transatlantic long-haul carriers have also shown large financial losses.

Passenger traffic grew more quickly on intra-European services than for world services as a whole, and partly for this reason B.E.A. was less badly affected. In 1971/72 the airline showed a profit of £181,000 after interest payments. However, during that year B.E.A. drew the last £8 million from the fund intended to reflect the higher operating costs of Trident 3 aircraft. Without this special grant, the airline would have shown a loss. At the time of writing, there is no indication that B.E.A. are to receive a further amount of compensation in respect of the higher operating costs of their British aircraft.

The adverse financial results experienced by airlines, especially long-haul airlines, has been only partly due to an imbalance between capacity and demand. Another major contributing factor has been the rapid growth of charter traffic which, it is estimated, increased by about 900 per cent over the 1960s. Though some two-thirds of the charter passengers were actually carried by schedule airlines operating charters, the combination of the growth of non-scheduled airlines and the low revenue from charter flights meant financial problems for the scheduled airlines. By the early 1970s there was also widespread infringement of charter regulations and some airlines, notably B.O.A.C., were pressing for cuts in schedule airfares on long-haul routes.

During the latter half of 1972, I.A.T.A. members agreed that fares must come down, but failed to agree on a fares package. The breakdown of talks has led to an 'open rate' situation under which airlines and Governments must fix the fares. B.O.A.C. is anxious to establish a low-fare advance booking system on its routes, and other proposals include non-bookable Transatlantic flights at very low prices. Though these proposals are approved by the Civil Aviation Authority, they must also obtain sanction from the licensing authorities of other countries who have power to deny landing rights. Thus the Transatlantic proposals must be approved by the U S Civil Aeronautic's Board or the Canadian authorities.

The open rate fares situation is a new development for the nationalized airlines to face, but there are other questions of importance. One, which has been discussed earlier, is the airlines' procurement policy. In the past year, both B.E.A. and B.O.A.C. have placed important orders for aircraft B.E.A. have chosen the Tristar to operate on its high capacity medium length routes during the mid-1970s, while B.O.A.C. have ordered five Concorde supersonic airliners. No details have yet been given of whether the operation of these aircraft will be compensated by the Government, though it would appear to be certain in the case of Concorde.

B.E.A.'s choice of the Tristar was particularly interesting since this wide-bodied jet would also be suitable for some of B.O.A.C.'s routes, and the issue was again raised of whether the two airlines should be merged. The British Airways Board in its first report made the point that 'the need for legally separate Air Corporations will be a matter for the Airways Board's early consideration.' As a result top management was centralised and a greater element of financial integration introduced. Route planning and aircraft re-equipment were vested in the Airways Board. In early 1973, the Board announced that the two state airlines were effectively to be merged and operate as divisions under the general title of British Airways, though retaining day to day autonomy. The Board believes that the financial benefit of tying B.O.A.C. and B.E.A. together would be some £100 million in the first five years and £40 million per annum thereafter.

References

Nationalized Industries and Public Enterprise: General

The Financial and Economic Objectives of the Nationalised Industries
    (1961), H.M.S.O., Cmnd 1337.
Nationalised Industries: A Review of Economic and Financial Objectives
    (1967), H.M.S.O., Cmnd 3437.

Fuel Industries and Policy

General

ECONOMIST INTELLIGENCE UNIT (1968), *Britain's Energy
    Supply*, E.I.U.
Fuel Policy (1967), H.M.S.O., Cmnd 3438.
SELECT COMMITTEE ON NATIONALISED INDUSTRIES (1968),
    Ministerial Control of the Nationalised Industries, H.M.S.O.,
    3 vols.

Electricity

MEEK, R. L. (1968), 'The new bulk supply tariff for electricity',
    Economic Journal, vol. 78, pp. 43–66.
NATIONAL BOARD FOR PRICES AND INCOMES (1968), Report
    no. 59, *Bulk Supply Tariff of the Central Electricity Generating
    Board*, H.M.S.O., Cmnd 3575.
*Report of the Committee of Enquiry into Delays in Commissioning
    C.E.G.B. Power Stations* (1969), H.M.S.O.. Cmnd 3960.
SELECT COMMITTEE ON NATIONALISED INDUSTRIES (1963),
    The Electricity Supply Industry, H.M.S.O.
TURVEY, R. (1968), *Optimal Pricing and Investment in Electricity
    Supply*, Allen & Unwin.
WATTS, P. E. (1968), 'C.E.G.B.'s bulk supply tariff and long-run
    marginal costs', *Economic Journal*, vol. 78, pp. 67–76.
WEBB, M. G. (1967), 'Some principles involved in the economic
    comparison of power stations', *Manchester School of Economic
    and Social Studies*, vol. 35, pp.1–18.

Gas

NATIONAL BOARD FOR PRICES AND INCOMES (1969), Report no. 102, *Gas Prices (Second Report)*, H.M.S.O., Cmnd 3974.

POLANYI, G. (1967), *What Price North Sea Gas?*, Hobart Paper no. 38, Institute of Economic Affairs.

SELECT COMMITTEE ON NATIONALISED INDUSTRIES (1961), *The Gas Industry*, H.M.S.O.

SELECT COMMITTEE ON NATIONALISED INDUSTRIES (1968), *The Exploitation of North Sea Gas*, H.M.S.O.

SELECT COMMITTEE ON NATIONALISED INDUSTRIES (1969), *The Exploitation of North Sea Gas: Observations by the Minister of Power*, H.M.S.O., Cmnd 3996.

Coal

CONFEDERATION OF BRITISH INDUSTRY, *Coal: The Price Structure 1966*.

PLATT, J. (1968), *British Coal*, Lyon, Grant & Green.

SELECT COMMITTEE ON NATIONALISED INDUSTRIES (1969), *National Coal Board*, H.M.S.O.

SHEPHERD, W. G. (1964), 'Cross-subsidising and allocation in public firms', *Oxford Economic Papers*, abridged as 'Cross-subsidization in coal' in R. Turvey (ed.) (1968), *Public Enterprise*, Penguin Books.

Transport

General

FOSTER, C. D. (1963), *The Transport Problem*, Blackie.

GWILLIAM, K. M. (1964), *Transport and Public Policy*, Allen & Unwin.

MINISTRY OF TRANSPORT (1967), *Transport of Freight*, H.M.S.O., Cmnd 3470.

MUNBY, D. (ed.) (1968), *Transport*, Penguin Books.

SAVAGE, C. I. (1966), *An Economic History of Transport*, Hutchinson.

SELECT COMMITTEE ON NATIONALISED INDUSTRIES (1968), *Ministerial Control of the Nationalised Industries*, H.M.S.O.

Transport Act 1968 (1968), H.M.S.O.

Railways

BRITISH RAILWAYS BOARD (1963), *The Reshaping of British Railways*: part 1, *Report*; part 2, *Maps*: H.M.S.O.

HARRISON, A. A. (1957), 'Railway freight charges', *Journal of the Institute of Transport*.

JOY, S. (1964), 'Railway track costs', *Journal of Industrial Economics*, reprinted in D. Munby (ed.) (1968), *Transport*, Penguin Books.

NATIONAL BOARD FOR PRICES AND INCOMES (1968), Report no. 72, *Proposed Increases by British Railways Board in Certain Country-Wide Fares and Charges*, H.M.S.O.

Railway Policy (1967), H.M.S.O., Cmnd 3439.

SELECT COMMITTEE ON NATIONALISED INDUSTRIES (1960), *British Railways*, H.M.S.O.

Road

NATIONAL BOARD FOR PRICES AND INCOMES (1965), Report no. 1, *Road Haulage Rates*, H.M.S.O., Cmnd 2695.

NATIONAL BOARD FOR PRICES AND INCOMES, Report (1967), no. 48, *Charges, Costs and Wages in the Road Haulage Industry*, H.M.S.O., Cmnd 3482.

NATIONAL BOARD FOR PRICES AND INCOMES (1968), Report no. 94, *Productivity Agreements in the Road Haulage Industry*, H.M.S.O., Cmnd 3847.

Report of the Committee on Carriers' Licensing (1965), Geddes Committee, H.M.S.O.

Airlines

EDWARDS COMMITTEE (1969), *British Air Transport in the Seventies*, H.M.S.O., Cmnd 4018.

GWILLIAM, K. M. (1966), 'The regulation of air transport', *Yorkshire Bulletin of Economic and Social Research*, vol. 18, pp. 20–33.

GWILLIAM, K. M. (1968), 'Domestic air transport fares', *Journal of Transport Economics and Policy*, vol. 2, pp. 203–17.

MINISTRY OF AVIATION (1963), *The Financial Problems of the British Overseas Airways Corporation*, H.M.S.O.

SELECT COMMITTEE ON NATIONALISED INDUSTRIES (1964), *British Overseas Airways Corporation*, H.M.S.O.

SELECT COMMITTEE ON NATIONALISED INDUSTRIES (1967), *British European Airways*, H.M.S.O.

WHEATCROFT, S. (1964), *Air Transport Policy*, Michael Joseph.

Further Reading

Nationalized Industries and Public Enterprise: General

HANSON, A. H. (ed.), *Nationalisation: A Book of Readings*,
  Allen & Unwin, 1963.
KELF-COHEN, R., *Twenty Years of Nationalisation*,
  Macmillan, 1969.
ROBSON, W. A., *Nationalised Industry and Public
  Ownership*, Allen & Unwin, 1960.
SELECT COMMITTEE ON NATIONALISED INDUSTRIES,
  Ministerial Control of the Nationalised Industries, H.M.S.O., 1968,
  3 vols.
SHANKS, M. (ed.), *The Lessons of Public Enterprise*, Cape, 1963.
THORNHILL, W., *The Nationalised Industries*, Nelson, 1968.
TIVEY, L., *Nationalisation in British Industry*, Cape, 1966.

Fuel Industries and Policy

General

DUNNING, J. H., and THOMAS, C. J., *British Industry*,
  Hutchinson, 1966, pp. 79–115.
Fuel Policy, H.M.S.O., 1965 Cmnd 2798.
JENSEN, W. G., *Energy in Europe 1945–1980*, Foulis 1967.
LITTLE, I. M. D., *The Price of Fuel*, Oxford University Press, 1953.
MANCHESTER JOINT RESEARCH COUNCIL, *Economic Aspects
  of Fuel and Power in British Industry*, Manchester
  University Press, 1960.
MINISTRY OF POWER, *Statistical Digest*, H.M.S.O., annual.
ORGANISATION FOR ECONOMIC CO-OPERATION AND
  DEVELOPMENT, *Statistics of Energy 1952–1966*,
  O.E.C.D., 1968.
POLITICAL AND ECONOMIC PLANNING, *Questions of
  Fuel Policy*, P.E.P., 1965.
POLITICAL AND ECONOMIC PLANNING, *A Fuel Policy for
  Britain*, P.E.P., 1966.

Report of the Committee on National Policy for the Use of Fuel and Power Resources, H.M.S.O., 1952, Cmnd 8647.

SELECT COMMITTEE ON NATIONALISED INDUSTRIES, *Gas, Electricity and Coal Industries*, H.M.S.O., 1966.

SIMPSON, E. S., *Coal and the Power Industries in Post-War Britain*, Longmans, 1966.

Electricity

AREA ELECTRICITY BOARDS, *Annual Reports and Accounts*, H.M.S.O.

BURN, D., *The Political Economy of Nuclear Energy*, Institute of Economic Affairs, 1967.

CENTRAL ELECTRICITY GENERATING BOARD, *Annual Reports and Accounts*, H.M.S.O.

HASSON, J. A., *The Economics of Nuclear Power*, Longmans, 1965.

NATIONAL BOARD FOR PRICES AND INCOMES, Report no. 7, *Electricity and Gas Tariffs*, H.M.S.O., 1965, Cmnd 2862.

NORTH OF SCOTLAND HYDRO-ELECTRIC BOARD, *Annual Reports and Accounts*, H.M.S.O.

ORGANISATION FOR ECONOMIC CO-OPERATION AND DEVELOPMENT, *The Electricity Supply Industry*, O.E.C.D., annual.

SCOTTISH DEVELOPMENT DEPARTMENT, *Electricity in Scotland*, H.M.S.O., 1962, Cmnd 1859.

SOUTH OF SCOTLAND ELECTRICITY BOARD, *Annual Reports and Accounts*, H.M.S.O.

THE ELECTRICITY COUNCIL, *Annual Reports and Accounts*, H.M.S.O.

WEBB, M. G., 'Some aspects of nuclear power economics in the United Kingdom', *Scottish Journal of Political Economy*, 1968, vol. 15, pp. 22–42.

Gas

AREA BOARDS, *Annual Reports and Accounts*, H.M.S.O.

GAS COUNCIL, *Annual Reports and Accounts*, H.M.S.O.

NATIONAL BOARD FOR PRICES AND INCOMES, Report no. 57, *Gas Prices (First Report)*, H.M.S.O., 1968, Cmnd 3567.

Coal

BEACHAM, A. 'The coal industry', in D. BURN (ed.), *The Structure of British Industry*, vol. 1, Cambridge University Press, 1958.

COURT, W. H. B., *Coal*, History of the Second World War, U.K. Civil Series, H.M.S.O. and Longmans, 1951.

NATIONAL COAL BOARD, *Plan for Coal*, H.M.S.O., 1950.

NATIONAL COAL BOARD, *Investing in Coal*, H.M.S.O., 1956.

NATIONAL COAL BOARD, *Revised Plan for Coal*, H.M.S.O., 1959.

NATIONAL COAL BOARD, *Annual Reports and Accounts*, H.M.S.O.
NATIONAL BOARD FOR PRICES AND INCOMES, Report no. 12,
  Coal Prices, H.M.S.O., 1966, Cmnd 2919.
UNITED NATIONS, *Consumption of Solid Fuels in the Domestic
  Sector*, U.N., 1967.
UNITED NATIONS, *The Coal Situation in Europe in 1966
  and its Prospects*, U.N., 1967.

Transport

General

BRITISH TRANSPORT COMMISSION, *Annual Reports and Accounts*,
  H.M.S.O., 1948–62.
Institute of Transport Journal, published six times a year.
Journal of Transport Economics and Policy, published three times a
  year.
MINISTRY OF TRANSPORT, *The Transport Needs of Great
  Britain in the Next Twenty Years*, H.M.S.O., 1963.
MINISTRY OF TRANSPORT, *Passenger Transport in Great
  Britain 1966*, H.M.S.O., 1968.
Public Transport and Traffic, H.M.S.O., 1967, Cmnd 3481.
RAY, G. F., and SAUNDERS, C. T., 'Problems and policies for inland
  transport', in W. Beckerman *et al.*, *The British Economy in 1975*,
  Cambridge University Press, 1965.
SARGENT, J. R., *British Transport Policy*, Oxford Univerity Press,
  1958.
SAVAGE, C. I., *Inland Transport*, History of the Second World War,
  U.K. Civil Series, H.M.S.O. and Longmans, 1957.
Transport Policy, H.M.S.O., 1966, Cmnd 3057.
WALKER, G., *Road and Rail*, Allen & Unwin, 1947.
WALTERS, A. A., *Integration in Freight Transport*, Institute of
  Economic Affairs, 1968.

Railways

ALDCROFT, D. H., *British Railways in Transition*, Macmillan, 1968.
ALLAN, G. F., *British Rail after Beeching*, Ian Allen, 1966.
BRITISH TRANSPORT COMMISSION, *Annual Reports and Accounts*,
  1948–62.
BRITISH TRANSPORT COMMISSION, *Modernisation and
  Re-equipment of British Railways*, H.M.S.O., 1955.
BRITISH TRANSPORT COMMISSION, *Modernisation Progress
  Report*. H.M.S.O., 1961.
BRITISH RAILWAYS BOARD, *Annual Reports and Accounts*,
  1963 onwards.

BRITISH RAILWAYS BOARD, *A Study of the Relative True Costs of Rail and Road Freight Transport over Trunk Routes*, H.M.S.O., 1964.

BRITISH RAILWAYS BOARD, *The Development of the Major Railway Trunk Routes*, H.M.S.O., 1965.

MINISTRY OF TRANSPORT, *British Railways Network for Development*, H.M.S.O., 1967.

MUNBY, D. L., 'Economic problems of British Railways', *Bulletin of the Oxford Institute of Statistics*, 1962, vol. 24, pp. 1–29.

MUNBY, D. L., 'The reshaping of British Railways', *Journal of Industrial Economics*, 1963, vol. 11, pp. 161–82.

Proposals for the Railways, H.M.S.O., 1956, Cmnd 9880.

Railways Reorganisation Scheme, H.M.S.O., 1954, Cmnd 9191.

Reappraisal of the Plan for the Modernisation and Re-equipment of British Railways, H.M.S.O., 1959, Cmnd 813.

SIMMONS, J., *The Railways of Britain*, Routledge & Kegan Paul, 1968.

SPECIAL REPORT FROM THE SELECT COMMITTEE ON NATIONALISED INDUSTRIES, *British Railways*, H.M.S.O., 1961.

Road

BRITISH TRANSPORT COMMISSION, *Annual Reports and Accounts*, 1948–62.

BRITISH ROAD FEDERATION, *Basic Road Statistics 1968*.

MINISTRY OF TRANSPORT, *Survey of Road Goods Transport 1968*, Final Results, part 1, H.M.S.O., 1964.

MINISTRY OF TRANSPORT, *Highway Statistics 1967*, H.M.S.O., 1968.

MINISTRY OF TRANSPORT, *Transport for Industry*, H.M.S.O., 1968.

NATIONAL FREIGHT CORPORATION, *Annual Reports and Accounts*, 1969 onwards.

TRANSPORT HOLDING COMPANY, *Annual Reports and Accounts*, 1963–8.

Airlines

AIR TRANSPORT LICENSING BOARD, *Annual Reports*.

BRITISH EUROPEAN AIRWAYS, *Annual Reports and Accounts*.

BRITISH OVERSEAS AIRWAYS CORPORATION, *Annual Reports and Accounts*.

FOLDES, L., 'Domestic air transport policy', *Economica*, 1961, vol. 28, pp. 156–75, 230–85.

Index

More about Penguins
and Pelicans

Penguinews, which appears every month, contains
details of all the new books issued by Penguins as they
are published. From time to time it is supplemented by
Penguins in Print, which is a complete list of all titles
available. (There are some five thousand of these.)
A specimen copy of *Penguinews* will be sent to you
free on request. For a year's issues (including the
complete lists) please send 50p if you live in the
British Isles, or 75p if you live elsewhere. Just write to
Dept EP, Penguin Books Ltd, Harmondsworth,
Middlesex, enclosing a cheque or postal order, and
your name will be added to the mailing list.

In the U.S.A.: For a complete list of books available
from Penguin in the United States write to Dept CS,
Penguin Books Inc., 7110 Ambassador Road,
Baltimore, Maryland 21207.

In Canada: For a complete list of books available
from Penguin in Canada write to Penguin Books
Canada Ltd, 41 Steelcase Road West, Markham,
Ontario.

The Economics of Industrial Innovation

Christopher Freeman

In the world of computers, space travel and energy crises we may curse or bless technical innovation, but we cannot escape its impact on our daily lives, nor the moral, social and economic dilemmas with which it confronts us. Least of all can economists afford to ignore innovation – an essential condition of economic progress and adaptation and a critical element in the competitive struggle of enterprises and nation states.

In Part One of his book, Professor Freeman illustrates historically three basic aspects of the rise of the professionalized Research and Development system – the growing complexity of technology, the increased scale of process, and the specialization of scientific work. The whole of Part Two is devoted to an examination of empirical evidence which might support or refute various contemporary theories of innovation, particularly in relation to the behaviour of firms. Part Three deals with some national-policy implications for technical innovation, and especially with the problem of 'consumer sovereignty'.

Monopoly and Competition

Edited by Alex Hunter

'People of the same trade', runs Adam Smith's famous remark, 'seldom meet together even for merriment and diversion but the conversation ends in a conspiracy against the public or in some contrivance to raise prices.' The problem is still with us in modern dress. Indeed, as the editor of this fascinating survey puts it, 'Not only are we examining the phenomenon of monopoly, oligarchy and merger from the wrong point of view, but the statutory tools we employ are already obsolete.'

In an area of thought in which objectives of economic efficiency tangle consistently with value judgements on the kind of society we wish to have, Dr Hunter is a meticulous guide. Part One indicates the progress of the more important developments in theory. Part Two brings out the manipulative techniques of economists. Part Three examines the particular difficulties of applying efficiently economic and organizational concepts through a process of law. Part Four quotes from judgements on problems of competition and monopoly.

Dr Alex Hunter is Professorial Fellow in Economics in the Research School of Social Science at the Australian National University.

Industrial Concentration

M. A. Utton

This book neatly considers the whole range of arguments for and against high levels of industrial concentration. Early chapters explain the factors governing level of and changes in concentration, and review the strengths and weaknesses of the measures that empirical studies have used. Three central chapters then follow: they form a survey of the available evidence on concentration levels and trends both in Britain and the United States, and are the core of the book. Included are such questions as whether concentration levels in the two countries have shown a persistent tendency to increase throughout the twentieth century.

In chapter 7 the author, emphasizing that his subject is useful only to the extent that it can indicate market performance, considers in particular whether profit levels in concentrated industries are significantly higher than in more competitive industries.

The final chapter considers the whole range of attitudes to concentration that governments may adopt in the search for better industrial performance.

Michael Utton is Lecturer in Economics at the University of Reading.